SAGE STERLING FOR WINDOWS
in easy steps

Ralf Kirchmayr

COMPUTER STEP

In easy steps is an imprint of Computer Step
5c Southfield Road, Southam
Warwickshire CV33 OJH England
☎01926 817999

SHEFFIELD
CITY LIBRARIES
cM
196-083089
OFC

First published 1996
Copyright © 1996 by Computer Step

All rights reserved. No part of this book may be reproduced or
transmitted in any form or by any means, electronic or mechanical,
including photocopying, recording, or by any information storage or
retrieval system, without prior written permission from the publisher.

Notice of Liability
Every effort has been made to ensure that this book contains accurate
and current information. However, Computer Step and the author
shall not be liable for any loss or damage suffered by readers as a
result of any information contained herein.

Trademarks
Microsoft$_®$ and Windows$_®$ are registered trademarks of Microsoft
Corporation. Sage Sterling, Bookkeeper, Accountant, Accountant
Plus and Financial Controller are all registered trademarks of The
Sage Group Plc. All other trademarks are acknowledged as belonging
to their respective companies.

Acknowledgements
Screenshots relating to Sage Sterling for Windows are included with
the kind permission of The Sage Group Plc.

For all sales and volume discounts please contact Computer Step on
Tel: 01926 817999.

For export orders and reprint/translation rights write to the address
above or Fax: (+44) 1926 817005.

Printed and bound in England

ISBN 1-874029-43-1

Contents

1. First Steps 7

Introduction 8
Starting Sterling for Windows 9
Company Setup 10
    Setting Up Tax Codes 11
    Setting Your Customer & Supplier Defaults 12
    Product, Currency & Control Accounts Defaults 13
Business Transactions 14
Sterling for Windows Iconbar 15
Entering Password 16

2. The Customer Ledger 17

The Purpose of Bookkeeping and Accounts 18
The Customer Iconbar 19
The Customer Record List 20
Invoices 21
Batch Invoices 22
Customer Activity 23
The Customer Aged Balance 24
The Customer Credit Note 25
Customer Mailing Labels & Letters 26
The Customer Statement 28
The Layout Designer 29
Customer Reports 30

3. The Supplier Ledger 31

The Supplier Iconbar 32
The Supplier Record List 33
The Supplier Invoice 34
The Supplier Activity 35
The Supplier Aged Balance 36
The Supplier Credit Note 37

The Supplier Mailing Labels and Letters 38

The Supplier Reports 40

4. The Nominal Ledger 41

The Nominal Ledger 42

The Nominal Iconbar 43

The Nominal Records 44

The Records Analysis 46

The Journal 48

    The Double-entry Principle 48

The Journal Double-entry 50

Prepayments 51

Accruals 52

The Chart of Accounts 53

Nominal Reports 56

5. The Bank 57

The Bank Account 58

The Bank Iconbar 60

Setting Up Bank Account Details 61

Recording Bank Payments 62

Credit Card Transactions 63

Cash Accounts 64

Cash Account Payments & Receipts 65

Supplier Payments 66

The Bank Receipt 67

The Customer Receipt 68

The Bank Account Transfer 69

Recurring Entries 70

The Bank Account Reconciliation 71

The Bank Statement 73

The Bank Reports 74

6. Products 75

The Product Record 76

The Products Iconbar 77

Product Record Details...78
   The Bill of Materials Tab 79
   The Sales Tab 79
   Product Graph View 80
   Viewing Product Activity..81
   Entering Product Discounts 81
Adjustments 82
Product Transfer 83
The Product Reports 84

7. Generating Invoices 85

The Invoice Iconbar 86
The Product Invoice 87
The Service Invoice 91
Printing Invoices 93
Skeleton Invoices 94
Generating Credit Notes 95
Updating The Ledgers 96
Deleting Invoices 97
Invoice Reports 98

8. Fixed Assets 99

The Fixed Assets Iconbar..100
Setting Up Fixed Assets 101
Asset Valuation 104

9. Financials 105

The Financials Iconbar..106
The Audit Trail 107
The Trial Balance 109
The Profit & Loss Report...110
The Balance Sheet 111
The Budget Report...112
The Prior Year Report 115
The VAT Return 116

10. The Report Generator 119

Running an Existing Report 120
Creating a New Report 121

11. Opening Balances 123

Introduction 124
    VAT Considerations 124
    Allocation Considerations 125
    Ageing Considerations 125
    When to Enter Opening Balances 125
Opening Balances and Standard VAT Scheme 126
Opening Balances and VAT Cash Accounting 129
No Full Opening Trial Balance 130

12. Period End 131

The Month End Procedure 132
The Year End Procedure 134
Clearing the Audit Trail and Stock 136

13. Data Management 137

Backing Up 138
Restore 140
Global Changes 141
Importing Data 143
Disk Doctor 145
    The Disk Doctor Iconbar 146
    Disk Doctor Check 146
    Disk Doctor Correct 147
    Disk Doctor Compress 148
    Disk Doctor Rebuild 148
Write Off, Refund, Return 149
Writing Off Bad Debts 152
Contra Entries 154

Index 155

First Steps

This chapter will get you started with Sage Sterling for Windows. It covers the initial startup procedures you will need to follow before you can start.

CHAPTER ONE

Covers

Introduction 8

Starting Sterling for Windows 9

Company Setup 10

Business Transactions... 14

Sterling for Windows Iconbar 15

Entering Password... 16

Introduction

Many people in business may one day decide to purchase a computer and by running some accounting program think that all their books will be dealt with. However, experience has shown that unless the person knows what he or she is doing, the records often end up in a mess.

What Can Sage Sterling for Windows Do for You?
In a clear, concise and easy to understand way this book will guide you through the most important steps that you will have to undertake in keeping your business accounts.

- Create and maintain your customer list and records, print invoices, credit notes and statements. Produce history reports.

- Create and maintain your supplier list and records, enter batch invoices and credit notes. Produce history reports.

- Maintain your Nominal Ledger and print those important management reports.

- Control your Bank, Credit Card and Cash accounts.

- Control your stock.

 Properly maintained accounts should reduce your accountancy fees.

Sage Sterling for Windows has a range of four products: Bookkeeper, Accountant, Accountant Plus and Financial Controller. All four products use the application, but with only certain options available depending on the level of product you purchased. Unfortunately, many of us are not very keen on "doing the books", but we all understand how important they are in running a prosperous business. A computer and the right software should help in several ways. It will tell you where your business stands financially and you will be able to make important decisions based on your monthly management reports.

Starting Sterling for Windows

Switch on your PC and your Windows desktop should be in front of you. If you are using Windows 3.x, then the Sage icon should appear in the Program Manager.

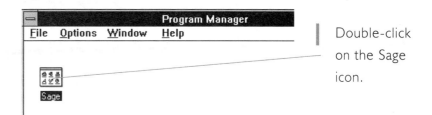

Double-click on the Sage icon.

2 Double-click on the Sterling for Windows icon.

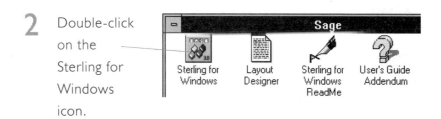

If you are using Windows 95 (or later) then the starting procedure will look like this:

3 Click here.

Click on the Start button.

2 Move your mouse pointer over "Sage".

Company Setup

If you are using Sterling for Windows for the first time then during the installation process you must enter your company details:

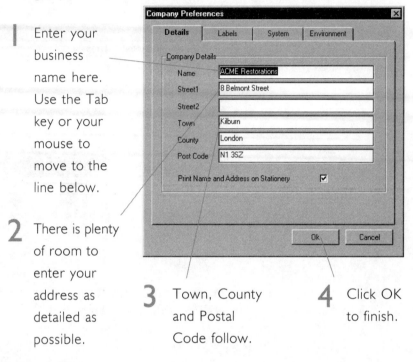

1 Enter your business name here. Use the Tab key or your mouse to move to the line below.

2 There is plenty of room to enter your address as detailed as possible.

3 Town, County and Postal Code follow.

4 Click OK to finish.

BEWARE

Ensure that you enter the correct starting month of your fiscal year. You will not be able to enter transactions before that month or after the end of that fiscal year.

These details can be changed when necessary by clicking on Defaults in the menu bar and choosing Company Preferences. To enter details of your financial year, do the following:

1 Click on Financial Year here.

2 Select the first month of your financial year from this list.

3 Click OK.

Setting Up Tax Codes

Choose Tax Codes after clicking on Details on the menu bar to enter or change VAT tax rates. The following codes are automatically set up during installation:

T0   –   zero rate transactions

T1   –   standard rate

T2   –   exempt transactions

T4   –   sales to customers in EC

T7   –   zero rated purchases from suppliers in EC

T8   –   standard rated purchases from suppliers in EC

T9   –   transactions not involving VAT

If unsure of the correct EU VAT tax rate then contact Customs & Excise.

1   Click on Tax Codes to display the list of codes and then click on the required code to bring up the Tax Code Setup. Make any necessary changes.

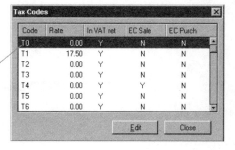

2   Enter percentage rate here.

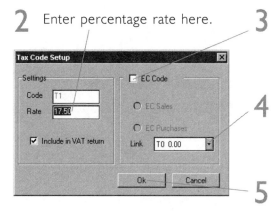

3   Check this box if VAT rate is for an EC code.

4   Link EC purchase code with selected tax code.

5   Click OK.

Setting Your Customer & Supplier Defaults

In Chapter Two customer records are discussed. Every time you create a new customer, details such as credit limit, discounts, etc. are required. First, however, you must enter your Customer Defaults.

HANDY TIP

Default nominal codes (N/C) for customers start at 4000 and for suppliers from 5000.

1 This tab lets you set the defaults which will appear on your customer records.

2 Set up Customer Statement, Aged Balances Period and Discount Defaults by clicking on the relevant tabs.

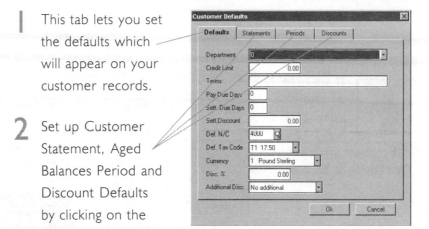

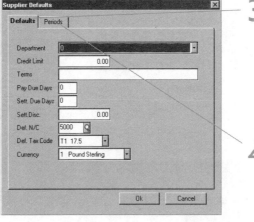

3 Do the same with your Supplier Defaults that will appear in your creditors records.

4 Use this tab to enter your Supplier Aged Balances Period.

...contd

Product, Currency & Control Accounts Defaults

Just as with Customer and Supplier Defaults, your Product records require defaults too.

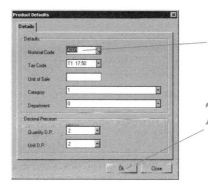

Use the Finder button to enter the Nominal Code or to create a new one.

1 Enter the correct Nominal account code here.

2 Click OK to save the information.

3 Control accounts are used by Sterling for Windows to make automatic double-entry postings.

You should not have to change the Control accounts unless you have created your own Chart of Accounts.

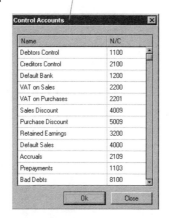

4 There are 99 different currencies to choose from. Click on the one required and then choose Edit.

Business Transactions

The term *business transaction* is easily defined as a person or persons performing the process of buying or selling goods or services in the view of earning a living or increasing financial gain.

As an example take a small business like the grocer on the street corner. In the morning you go there to purchase the daily newspaper, some milk and bread and for those goods you hand over some money to pay for them. The shopkeeper accepts the money and puts it into his till. At that moment your first transaction of the day has been performed. But as far as the shopkeeper is concerned there are several other business transactions that will have to be completed before he can close his shop and be assured that there is money left over in the till for the next day.

All the goods that he sold that day were supplied by many of his trade suppliers and all of them agreed to give the shopkeeper 30 days' credit on his account. That way the goods can be marketed and sold before they are actually paid for. So when it comes to the end of the month the shopkeeper sits down and writes a cheque to each of his suppliers to pay for the goods that have been supplied to him that month. Again, by doing that the shopkeeper is performing more business transactions.

When a cheque is written there is no cash being exchanged, unlike when the customer walked into the shop and paid for the goods that he bought. Therefore, from now on we will refer to money as a certain *value* of that *business transaction*.

Once the program has been loaded, the Sterling for Windows desktop appears.

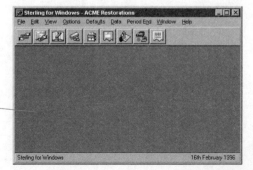

Sterling for Windows Iconbar

The Sterling for Windows iconbar offers the following functions, which can also be accessed from the menu bar by clicking on "Options" and then clicking on the required menu item.

HANDY TIP

Move the mouse pointer over the required icon and the description will display itself.

1 Open the Customer (sales) Ledger.

2 Open the Supplier (purchase) Ledger.

3 Open the Nominal (general) Ledger.

4 Open the Bank, Credit Card and Petty Cash accounts.

5 Open the Product Records and Stock accounts.

6 Generate invoices and credit notes.

7 Open the Financials window (i.e., Trial Balance, Profit & Loss).

8 Open the Fixed Assets window.

9 Open the Report Generator window.

Entering Password

As prescribed by the Data Protection Act you will be required to enter a password in case you hold detailed information about your customers and suppliers. Once a password has been entered Sterling for Windows will prompt you at startup.

1 From the menu bar click on Defaults.

2 Then move the mouse pointer over the Change Password option and click once.

REMEMBER

The New Password cannot be saved unless it's exactly the same as the Confirm New Password.

3 The Change Password window will appear.

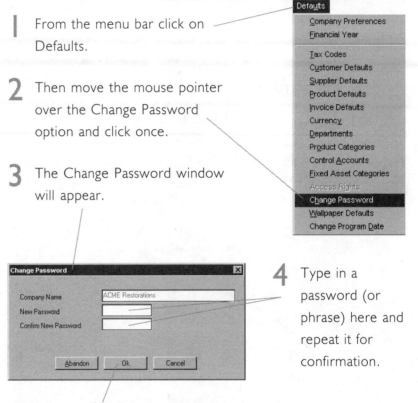

| Defaults |
| Company Preferences |
| Financial Year |
| Tax Codes |
| Customer Defaults |
| Supplier Defaults |
| Product Defaults |
| Invoice Defaults |
| Currency |
| Departments |
| Product Categories |
| Control Accounts |
| Fixed Asset Categories |
| Access Rights |
| Change Password |
| Wallpaper Defaults |
| Change Program Date |

Change Password

Company Name   ACME Restorations
New Password
Confirm New Password

Abandon   Ok   Cancel

4 Type in a password (or phrase) here and repeat it for confirmation.

5 When satisfied click OK, or Abandon to start again.

As with your credit card PIN number you should not write your password or pass phrase down unless absolutely necessary. You can increase the security by using a pass phrase that includes a "–" or "/" and combining alphanumeric (letters & numbers) characters. This will hinder any intruders attempting to find the correct combination by chance.

CHAPTER TWO

The Customer Ledger

This chapter will discuss the Customer (sales) Ledger, how to create and maintain new and existing customer records, and how to enter invoices and credit notes. It also covers how to maintain aged balances and analyse your customers' transaction history.

Covers

The Purpose of Bookkeeping & Accounts 18

The Customer Iconbar 19

The Customer Record List 20

Invoices 21

Batch Invoices 22

Customer Activity 23

The Customer Aged Balance 24

The Customer Credit Note 25

Customer Mailing Labels & Letters 26

The Customer Statement 28

The Layout Designer 29

Customer Reports 30

The Purpose of Bookkeeping and Accounts

Every business needs to keep some sort of record noting every business transaction, in order to create a picture of the current financial situation. Even some private individuals keep some sort of record of their finances so that they know what they can afford.

Properly maintained books will give you an estimation of your sales or liabilities for a certain period in the future.

This is particularly important should you require some financial assistance from your bank. When you ask for a loan or an overdraft to help you over a difficult time, the bank manager will want to see your business records so that he can judge if the business has a good enough cash flow to be able to carry another liability.

The Inland Revenue will require complete documentation of your business transactions so that your tax liability can be worked out. Then there is Customs & Excise and you will have to prove that you have calculated the correct VAT liability.

For all these bodies to be able to understand your books, the recording of business transactions and the rules of bookkeeping are universal. It is a language that every business manager will understand.

But most importantly you should keep proper books for one reason and that is to be able to produce monthly management reports so that you understand where the business stands financially in the present or future. On such information you then base your management decisions so that you can maximize your profits at the end of the business period.

The Customer Iconbar

The Customer iconbar provides features such as invoicing, credit notes and reporting.

HANDY TIP

Move the mouse pointer over the required **icon and the description will display itself.**

1   Open the Customer Records.

2   Open the Customer Activity.

3   Open the Customer Aged Balances

4   Open the Customer Batch Invoices input.

5   Open the Customer Credit Note input.

6   Open the Customer Telephone option.

7   Open the Customer Mailing Labels.

8   Open the Customer Letters.

9   Open the Customer Statements.

10   Open the Customer Reports.

The Customer Record List

The first icon option on the desktop is the Customer (sales) Ledger. Within this ledger you can perform the following actions:

- Maintain customer records and their details.

- Record invoices and credit notes that you have sent to your customers.

- Print customer statements.

- Analyse your customers' transaction history through reports, graphs and tables.

- Generate customer letters and mailing labels.

Once a transaction has been posted in your customer record, it can no longer be deleted.

After clicking on the Customer icon the Customers desktop will appear.

2 The first icon on the left is the Customer Record icon.

Be as detailed as possible with your customer record input.

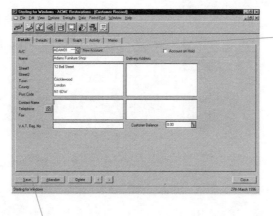

3 The Customer Record window appears and you must enter details to create a new customer, starting with the account code (A/C).

4 Click on Save to make the information permanent.

Invoices

When a business wants to record a sales or purchase transaction involving goods intended for resale, two different types of categories, cash and credit purchases, must be considered. If you have a cash transaction, where goods were paid for straight away, then you must debit the Purchase account and credit the Cash or Bank account. But in most cases a business will arrange to purchase their goods for resale on account from their supplier. That can be any period between 30 and 120 days. Therefore once goods are purchased your business has incurred a debt and your supplier has become your creditor.

At the same time you may sell goods to your customers on account and in this case they will become debtors of your business, the double-entry being a credit entry in your Sales account and a debit entry in your Cash or Bank account in the case of an immediate sale.

When a sale or purchase on account is being transacted, an invoice is raised informing the recipient of his or her debt.

The invoice will include the following details: an invoice number, the date the purchase was made, the price and description of the goods, any VAT added (if applicable) and the terms agreed upon (usually 30 days). Also the supplier's business details and the customer's address should be included. Usually there is also an order number as reference in case a purchase order was raised.

In Chapter Seven the immediate raising of product and service invoices is discussed, but if you use different software to create your invoices then the sales transaction input has to be made via the Batch Invoices option from the Customer Ledger.

Batch Invoices

As mentioned in the Invoices section previously, the Batch Invoices window is used to input a number of sales transactions for which invoices have been raised.

1 First move the mouse pointer over the Batch Invoices icon and click once with the left button.

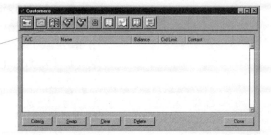

2 The Customer Batch Invoices window appears.

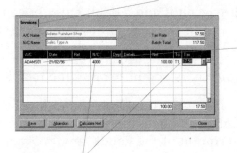

3 Type in the customer account code (A/C) or click on the Display icon just to the right of it to open the Customer List window.

4 Note the nominal account (N/C) default, and enter a description and amount. The tax code (Tc) is automatically set at T1 (calculating VAT at 17.5%). In case of no VAT, change this code to T9.

5 Click on Save, and the invoice is posted. After closing the window the Customer List will display the customer's latest balance.

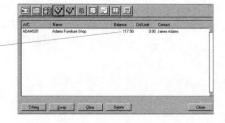

Customer Activity

The Customer Activity window will display the individual debit and credit entries made within a chosen customer account. Every debit entry refers to an invoice raised, and every credit entry refers to an invoice paid.

HANDY TIP

Customers who have reached their credit limit are displayed in red.

1 From the Customer List click on the account whose activity you want to look at.

2 Then click on the Activity icon.

3 The next window appearing will ask you to enter ranges for transaction numbers and/or dates.

4 Click OK.

HANDY TIP

To the far right of the Activity window, figures such as Balance, Amount Paid and Turnover YTD (Year-to Date), can be useful information.

5 The Customer Activity window will be displayed. Note the credit period and the aged balance.

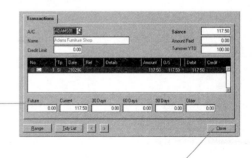

6 Click Close to finish.

The Customer Aged Balance

In the Customer Activity section aged balances were mentioned. These refer to the time elapsed between goods being sold and the outstanding debt of your customer. The average time of credit given by most businesses is 30 days, but they can be negotiated to longer periods such as 60 days or even longer. Some businesses even charge interest on outstanding invoices.

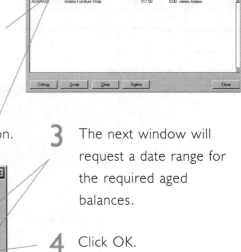

1 From the Customer List window click on the required customer for whom you want to request an aged balance.

HANDY TIP

Maximise the Aged Balances window to display the Older column.

2 Click on the Aged icon.

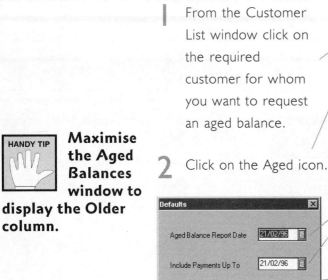

3 The next window will request a date range for the required aged balances.

4 Click OK.

5 This window will inform you of your customers' aged balances due.

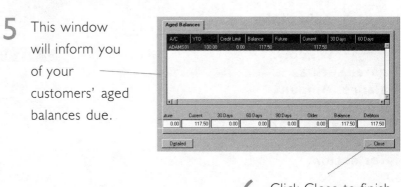

6 Click Close to finish.

The Customer Credit Note

Sometimes when supplying goods to your customers, the goods could be faulty and returned to you. Or the number of items dispatched could be less than ordered.

Instead of correcting the payment due to the correct amount you may issue a credit note to your customer. This may be a piece of paper not very different from the original invoice. It will carry the heading "Credit Note" and state the amount that you owe to your customer. Credit notes used to be printed in the colour red, but now businesses can print from a computer using black ink.

As with raising immediate invoices, credit notes can be raised and printed straight away. This is covered in Chapter Seven. If you produce credit notes within another system then the transaction can be recorded in the Customer Ledger.

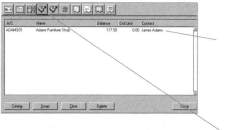

I From the Customer List window click on the customer for whom you want to issue a credit note.

2 Click on the Customer Credit Note icon.

REMEMBER

Look at the Customer List and it will display a new outstanding balance, the previous amount being reduced by the credit amount.

3 This input is the same as with batch invoices, using only the credited amount. Set the tax code (Tc) as T1 if required.

4 Click Save to post the transaction.

Customer Mailing Labels & Letters

Two very useful options provide preformatted letters and mailing labels for correspondence to your customers. There is a letter for outstanding payments due, but if you send those reminders on a regular basis your customers will get to know your system and will refrain from making payments till such a letter is received in the post.

If your system uses a voice modem, it's easiest to use the Telephone option to call your customers direct and chase any payments due.

Click on the Labels icon and the next window will offer you a choice of two different types of layout. Click on the one you need and then choose the output: Printer, Preview or File.

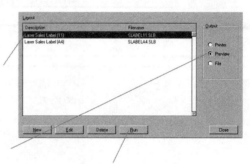

2 Click the Run button to create the output.

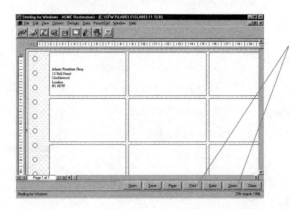

3 Once you are satisfied that the output is correct click the Print button. Use the Zoom button to zoom in or out of the page.

...contd

 The Telephone option will not work unless you have a communications port configured to your system.

4 Click on the Letters icon, and the next window will display a list of different layouts.

5 Click on the required layout and choose the required output (Printer, Preview or File).

6 Click the Run button.

7 Once satisfied you have the correct letter, choose the Print option. You can use the Zoom button to zoom in and out to get a better look at the document.

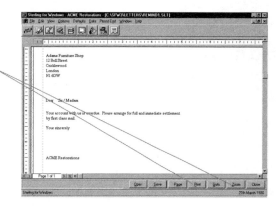

 HANDY TIP

Use the New or Edit button to work on your own letters.

The Customer Statement

At the end of every month the supplier of goods may want to issue a statement to inform his customers how their account stands in his books. It will list the invoices raised that month and ensure that the customer has received them. It can also clarify certain problems should an error have occurred during that business period.

Most of us at one time or another have made a purchase on credit and you could have seen many different styles of invoices, credit notes and statements. As long as they show all the relevant details mentioned earlier, it does not matter how they are designed. Using Sage Sterling for Windows you have the option to design your own documents to suit your own needs.

 Be sure to use the correct layout to fit the chosen stationery.

From the Customer menu, click on the Statement icon and in the next window select the required statement layout.

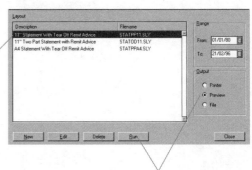

2 After choosing the correct layout and output options (Printer, Preview or File), click Run.

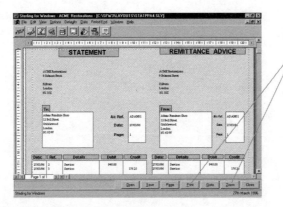

3 Click the Zoom button to zoom in or out. When satisfied click Print.

The Layout Designer

The Layout Designer lets you easily design new output files or change existing ones.

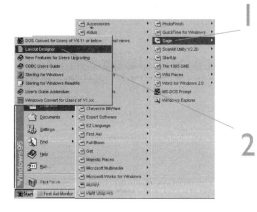

1 Move the mouse pointer to Start and click. Then move the mouse pointer over Sage.

2 Click on Layout Designer to start the program.

3 After clicking on the File menu, choose the Open option.

4 Choose the layout file you want to change.

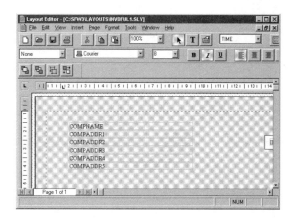

5 Now you can start to make the necessary changes. Don't forget to save the file before you exit the program.

Customer Reports

Start the Customer Reports option by clicking on the Reports icon within the Customer Ledger. There are already a large number of predesigned reports available that should cover most of your needs.

1 Move the mouse pointer over the required report and click.

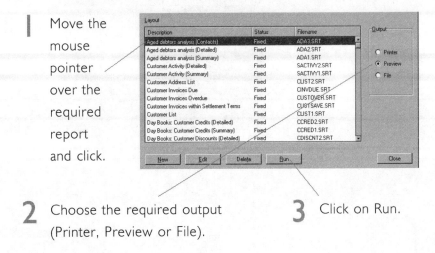

2 Choose the required output (Printer, Preview or File).

3 Click on Run.

CHAPTER THREE

The Supplier Ledger

This chapter will discuss the Supplier (purchase) Ledger and how to create and maintain new and existing suppliers, enter invoices and credit notes. It also covers how to maintain aged balances and analyse your supplier transaction history.

Covers

The Supplier Iconbar 32

The Supplier Record List 33

The Supplier Invoice 34

The Supplier Activity 35

The Supplier Aged Balance 36

The Supplier Credit Note 37

The Supplier Mailing Labels & Letters 38

The Supplier Reports 40

The Supplier Iconbar

The Supplier iconbar is similar to the Customer iconbar, providing the same features such as invoicing, credit notes and reporting.

   Open the Supplier Records.

   Open the Supplier Activity.

 HANDY TIP **Move the mouse pointer over the required icon and the description will display itself.**

   Open the Supplier Aged Balances.

   Open the Supplier Batch Invoices input.

   Open the Supplier Credit Note input.

   Open the Supplier Telephone option.

   Open the Supplier Mailing Labels.

  Open the Supplier Letters.

   Open the Supplier Reports.

1   2   3   4   5   6   7   8   9

The Supplier Record List

The second icon option on the desktop is the Supplier (purchase) Ledger. Within this ledger you can perform the following actions:

- Maintain supplier records and their details.

- Record invoices and credit notes that you have received from your suppliers.

- Analyse your suppliers' transaction history through reports, graphs and tables.

- Generate supplier letters and mailing labels.

BEWARE **Once a transaction has been posted in your supplier record, it can no longer be deleted.**

1 After clicking on the Supplier icon, the Supplier desktop will appear.

2 The first icon on the left is the Supplier Record icon. Click here.

HANDY TIP **Type as many details as possible into the supplier record.**

3 The Supplier Record window appears and you must enter details to create a new supplier, starting with the account code (A/C).

4 Click on Save to retain this information.

The Supplier Invoice

As mentioned in the Invoices section in Chapter Two, the Supplier Invoices (Batch Invoices) window is used to input a number of purchase transactions for which invoices have been received.

1 First move the mouse pointer over the Batch Invoices icon and click once with the left button.

2 The Batch Supplier Invoices window appears.

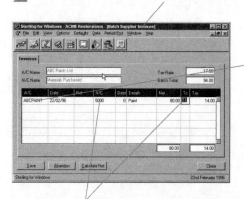

3 Type in the supplier's account code (A/C) or click on the Finder button just to the right of it to open the Supplier List window.

4 Note the nominal account (N/C) default, and enter a description and amount. The tax code (Tc) is automatically set at T1 (calculating VAT at 17.5%). In case of no VAT, change this code to T9.

5 After clicking on Save the invoice is posted and after closing the window the Supplier List will display the supplier's latest balance.

The Supplier Activity

The Supplier Activity window will display the individual debit and credit entries made within a chosen supplier account. Every credit entry refers to an invoice received and every debit entry refers to an invoice paid.

1 From the Supplier List click on the account of the supplier whose activity you want to look at.

2 Then click on the Activity icon.

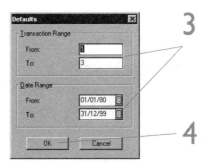

3 The next window will ask you to enter ranges for transaction numbers and/or dates.

4 Click OK.

HANDY TIP

To the far right of the Activity window, figures such as **Balance, Amount Paid and Turnover YTD (Year-to Date), can provide useful information.**

5 The supplier's activity will be displayed. Note the credit period and the aged balance.

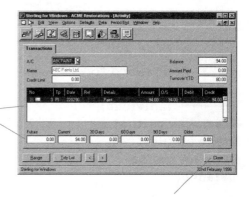

6 Click Close to finish.

The Supplier Aged Balance

In the Supplier Activity section aged balances were mentioned. These refer to the time elapsed between goods being bought and the outstanding debt to your supplier. The average period of credit given by most businesses is 30 days, but they can be negotiated to longer periods such as 60 or 90 days. Some businesses even charge interest on outstanding invoices.

I From the Supplier List window click on the supplier for whom you want to request an aged balance.

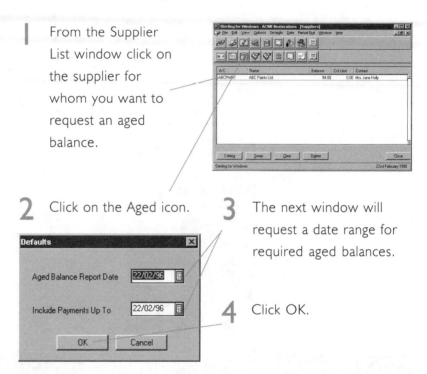

2 Click on the Aged icon.

3 The next window will request a date range for required aged balances.

4 Click OK.

HANDY TIP

Click on Detailed to look up individual transactions that make up the supplier's aged balance.

5 This window will inform you of your supplier's aged balances due.

6 Click Close to finish.

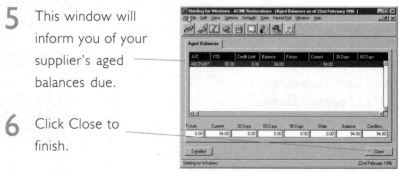

The Supplier Credit Note

Sometimes when purchasing goods from your supplier, the goods could be faulty and returned to him. Or the number of items dispatched could be less than you ordered.

Instead of correcting the payment due to the correct amount you may receive a credit note from your supplier. This may be a piece of paper not very different from the original invoice. It will carry the heading "Credit Note" and state the amount that your supplier owes you. Credit notes used to be printed in the colour red, but now businesses can print from a computer using black ink.

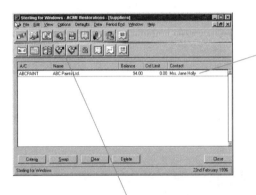

From the Supplier List window click on the name of the supplier from whom you have received a credit note.

2 Click on the Batch Credits icon.

HANDY TIP

Look at the Supplier List and it will display a new outstanding balance, the previous amount being reduced by the credit amount.

3 This input is the same as with batch invoices, using only the credited amount. Note the tax code (Tc) at T1 if required.

4 Click Save to post the transaction.

The Supplier Mailing Labels and Letters

Two very useful options provide preformatted letters and mailing labels for correspondence to your suppliers.

Click on the Labels icon and the next window will offer you a choice of two different types of layouts. Click on the one you need and then choose the required output.

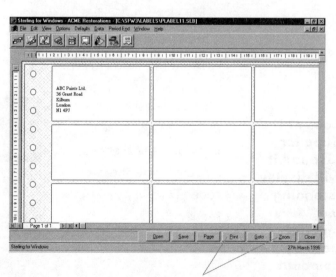

2 Click the Run button to create the output.

3 Once you are satisfied that the output is correct click the Print button. Use the Zoom button to zoom in or out of the page.

...contd

 The Telephone option will not work unless you have a communications port configured to your system.

4 Click on the Letters icon, and the next window will display a Change of Address layout.

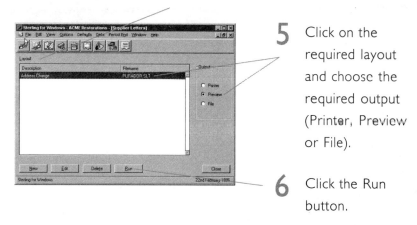

5 Click on the required layout and choose the required output (Printer, Preview or File).

6 Click the Run button.

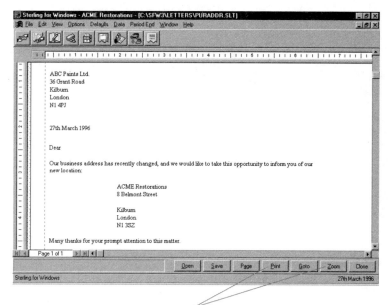

 Use the New or Edit button to work on your own letters.

7 Once satisfied that everything is in order choose the Print option. You can use the Zoom button to zoom in and out.

The Supplier Reports

Start the Supplier Report option by clicking on the Reports icon within the Supplier Ledger. There are already a large number of predesigned reports available that should cover most of your needs.

1 Move the mouse pointer over the required report and click.

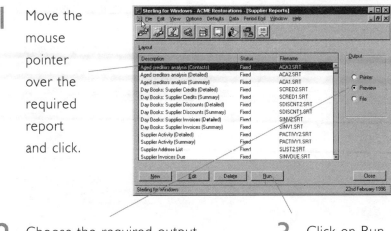

2 Choose the required output (Printer, Preview or File).

3 Click on Run.

CHAPTER FOUR

The Nominal Ledger

This chapter will discuss the Nominal (general) Ledger and how to create and maintain new and existing Nominal accounts. The analysis of individual accounts using graphs and reports will also be covered.

Covers

The Nominal Ledger 42

The Nominal Iconbar 43

The Nominal Records 44

The Records Analysis 46

The Journal 48

The Journal Double-entry 50

Prepayments 51

Accruals 52

The Chart of Accounts 53

Nominal Reports 56

The Nominal Ledger

The Nominal Ledger, also known as the General Ledger, is very different to the Sales and Purchase Ledgers. The Sales Ledger will inform you of details relating to your sales and the Purchase Ledger to purchases made from your suppliers.

The individual sales and purchases are then pooled into certain sales and purchase Nominal accounts. The management reporting programs will extract and use figures from those accounts to tell you how your business is performing at any given time. More about that in the Financials chapter.

Click on the Nominal icon to open the Nominal Ledger.

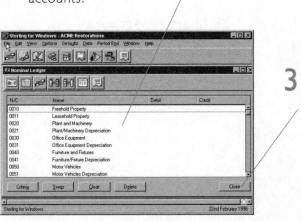

2 The Nominal Ledger opens and displays all existing Nominal accounts.

REMEMBER

The Accounts List in the Nominal Ledger is equal to the Chart of Accounts.

3 Click Close to leave the Nominal Ledger.

The Nominal Iconbar

The Nominal iconbar provides features such as account record maintenance, journal double-entries, prepayments and accruals, and analysis based on graphs and/or reports.

1 Open the Nominal Records.

2 Open the Nominal Activity.

3 Enter Nominal Ledger journal double-entries.

HANDY TIP **Move the mouse pointer over the required icon and the description will display itself.**

4 Enter Prepayments.

5 Enter Accruals.

6 Open the Nominal Chart of Accounts.

7 Open the Nominal Reports.

The Nominal Records

Why maintain a General Ledger? When many people in business are approached and asked why they are in business, the reply is, "To make money."

Others will have said, "To make a profit," and although some of us could argue and say that is the same thing we must realise that they are two very different concepts. The reason for this is quite simple. Every business will "make money", but not every business will make a profit.

As soon as you walk into the grocer's shop and purchase goods the shopkeeper has made money. But as mentioned earlier, the shopkeeper will still have to pay for the goods sold, the idea being that he will have sold the goods for more money than he had to pay for them. At the end of the day he has money left over in the till which at that time he considers to be a profit.

But there is, of course, more to profit and we will talk about that in the Financials chapter. At this stage we will consider that we perform business transactions with a view to create a maximised profit over a certain business period.

Let us start with the individual records. When you installed Sterling for Windows you may have chosen to use the default Chart of Accounts or you may have created your own. There are already a couple of transactions that we have entered earlier when using the Customer and Supplier Ledgers.

Using the scroll bar, move down the list of accounts and then select the Sales Type A account by clicking on it.

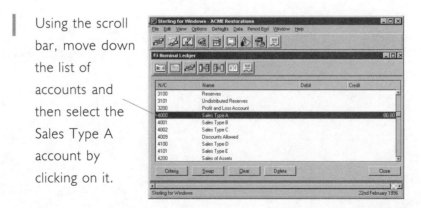

...contd

3 Click on the Records icon.

2 Once you click on the account it will be highlighted in blue.

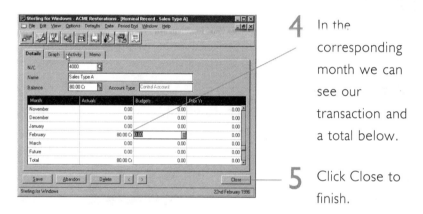

HANDY TIP

It is best to change the Sales account name to suit your needs.

4 In the corresponding month we can see our transaction and a total below.

5 Click Close to finish.

The first part of this window will only display the total value of transactions for each month with a cumulative total at the bottom. To the right of each monthly total a budget value can be entered, which will be used to create budget and ratio reports.

HANDY TIP

You can change the budgets at any time using the Global Changes feature from the Data menu.

At the top you will notice that this account is a control account and that is because it is linked with the Customer (sales) Ledger.

The Records Analysis

The other parts of the Nominal Record window can be very useful to analyse a particular account.

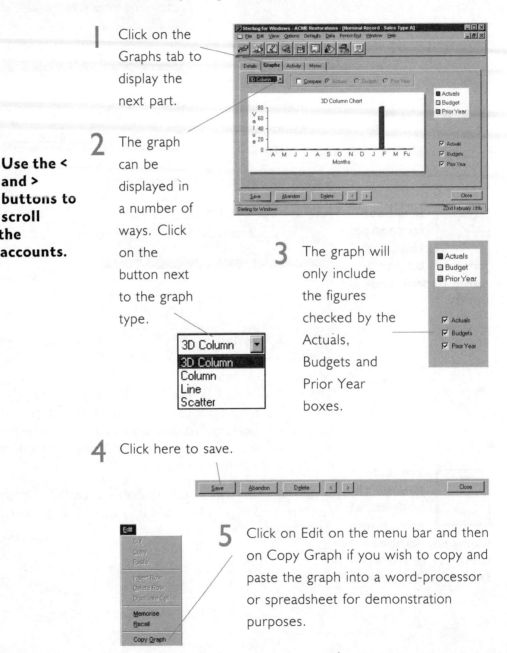

1   Click on the Graphs tab to display the next part.

HANDY TIP

Use the < and > buttons to scroll through the selected accounts.

2   The graph can be displayed in a number of ways. Click on the button next to the graph type.

3   The graph will only include the figures checked by the Actuals, Budgets and Prior Year boxes.

4   Click here to save.

5   Click on Edit on the menu bar and then on Copy Graph if you wish to copy and paste the graph into a word-processor or spreadsheet for demonstration purposes.

The Activity Window in the Record Analysis

This window will show the transaction history of a chosen account.

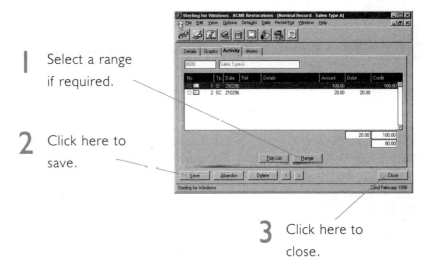

1 Select a range if required.

2 Click here to save.

3 Click here to close.

This window will allow you to write memos in case there are special requirements for the maintenance of an account.

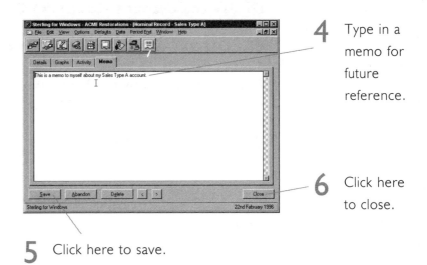

4 Type in a memo for future reference.

6 Click here to close.

5 Click here to save.

The Journal

The journal allows you to perform manual double-entries in case there is a transaction required that is not covered by any of the features of Sterling for Windows. Unless you have have some understanding about double-entry bookkeeping, this area could present problems.

The Double-entry Principle

As the word "bookkeeping" implies, your transactions are recorded in a book of some kind, and double-entry bookkeeping means that there is a double entry for each transaction in your book.

The main book in which you make your entries is called a "ledger". Those ledgers used to be thick books or loose leaves in a binder, but today they exist in the form of computerised data files.

Anyone who has seen the double-entry format in a ledger before may have noted that there are two sides to it. The left side is always referred to as the "Debit" side and the right is always referred to as the "Credit" side. There is an easy rule that you should remember:

DEBIT the account RECEIVING the value

CREDIT the account GIVING the value

As an example, let us think of buying something in a shop. I am your customer and for the goods that I am buying I am GIVING you some money. On the other hand, you, the shopkeeper, are selling those goods to me and you are RECEIVING the money I just gave you.

Therefore, every transaction must have two sides to it. Whatever value is given must also be received. When it is time for you to record the transaction of your sale, you will credit your Sales account (i.e., your Customer account) and debit your Bank account, which will be the final recipient of that money.

When the transaction is a purchase on credit, meaning an invoice has been raised, then instead of debiting the Bank account the Debtors Control account is the receiver of that value. There that value will remain until payment has been received, and then the Debtors Control account is the giver of that value (credit entry) and the Bank account is the receiver (debit entry).

This can cause some confusion, because we are used to saying that we have a "credit" in the bank, meaning we are in the black. Why is it that we record our deposit transaction as a debit entry?

The answer is that your bank is a separate entity to your business and you are their customer. The bank statements you receive from them are a copy of their Customer account and that is why it shows you as the giver of that value, resulting in a credit entry.

Click on the Journal button.

2 The Journal Entry window appears.

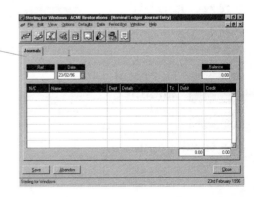

The Journal Double-entry

Here is how you would enter a journal entry for a sale of £100 deposited in the Bank account.

1 Enter a reference here. This entry is optional.

2 Enter the transaction date here.

3 Enter the Nominal account number (N/C) of the first account here.

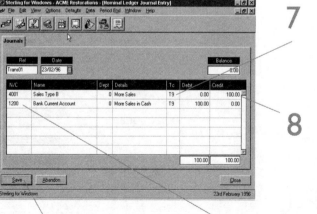

HANDY TIP

The tax code (Tc) will always be T9, unless the transaction involves the Sales or Purchase Tax Control account. Then it must be changed to T1. If not, the VAT Return program will not recognize it.

4 The account name is displayed automatically.

5 Enter the department number.

6 Enter a description.

7 The tax code will default to T9.

8 Enter either a debit or a credit amount.

REMEMBER

The total amount of debits must equal the total amount of credits.

10 Click Save to post.

9 Enter the double entry on the second line.

Prepayments

Sometimes revenue income and expenses may not have been received or paid for within the set accounting period when the reports are prepared. In the case of sales to Customer accounts and purchases relating to Supplier accounts, the Debtors and Creditors Control accounts will inform you of any outstanding debts or payments owed.

But what happens when, for example, you have made a payment, such as rent, that will also fall into the next accounting period as an expense? Let us say that you produce monthly management reports and your rent payments are made quarterly at £900. That clearly shows that your monthly rental liability is £300, but you have paid the total amount in the first month.

If you make a bank payment of £900 in the first month, the Profit & Loss statement will show it accordingly, and in the other two months it will account for no rental expense at all. Therefore, the Current Asset account called "Prepayments" is used. In it you can specify the total expense and what period it covers. When the Month End procedure is run, the correct monthly amount is posted to the Rental Expense account. All that is left to do is to post a bank payment to the Prepayments account for the full amount.

HANDY TIP
Use the Finder button to choose the Nominal account.

HANDY TIP
Use the Copy option in the Edit menu to duplicate rows.

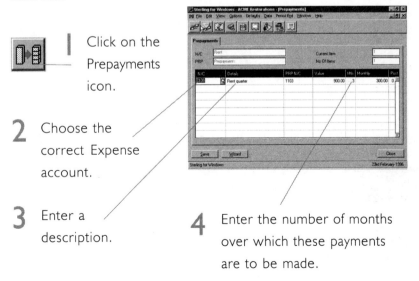

1 Click on the Prepayments icon.

2 Choose the correct Expense account.

3 Enter a description.

4 Enter the number of months over which these payments are to be made.

Accruals

Something similar to a prepayment occurs when an expense for the current period is not paid till the next accounting period. This time you use the Liability account called "Accruals". It works the same way as prepayments, only in reverse.

For example, let us say that the electricity bill was paid in one accounting period, but the charges fell into the previous period. The transaction is made using the Accrual and Electricity accounts when the charge actually fell due. When payment was made, the bank transaction was applied to the Accrual account, rather than to the Electricity account.

I Click on the Accruals icon.

HANDY TIP

Click on the Wizard to help you set up your accruals.

2 The Accruals window will appear.

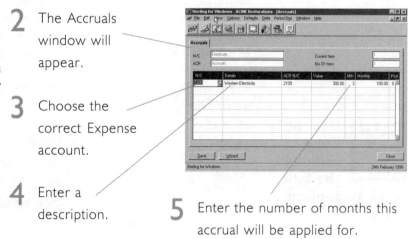

3 Choose the correct Expense account.

4 Enter a description.

5 Enter the number of months this accrual will be applied for.

This accrual will only be applied once the Month End procedure is run. See Chapter Twelve.

The Chart of Accounts

Sterling for Windows has already created a default Chart of Accounts when installing the program, suitable for the following financial reports:

*   The Profit & Loss Report

*   The Balance Sheet Report

*   The Budget Report

*   The Prior Year Report

These reports will be discussed in Chapter Nine, "Financials".

 1 Click on the Chart of Accounts icon.

2 The Chart of Accounts defaults window will appear.

3 Choose the required default Chart of Accounts.

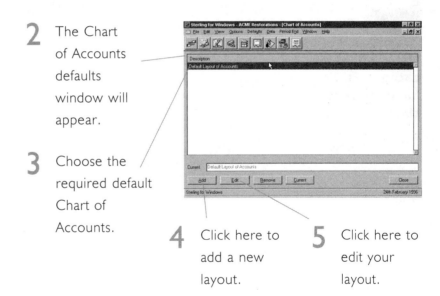

4 Click here to add a new layout.

5 Click here to edit your layout.

The Chart of Accounts Dialog Box

1 Click on the required category.

2 Change the description of the category if required in the report layout.

If you created your own Chart of Accounts layout there will be no categories. You will have to create them.

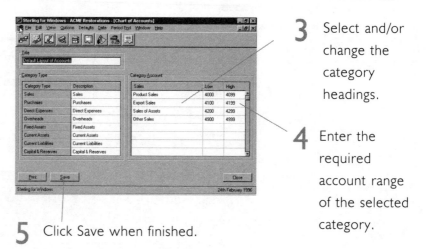

3 Select and/or change the category headings.

4 Enter the required account range of the selected category.

5 Click Save when finished.

Each category can be laid out as detailed as possible, choosing selected account ranges. This will be beneficial when you're looking at the financial reports generated to help you make business management decisions.

...contd

Printing Your Chart of Accounts

HANDY TIP

Print if you have created your own Chart of Accounts in case you have missed something.

1 Click on Print.

2 The Print Chart of Accounts window will appear.

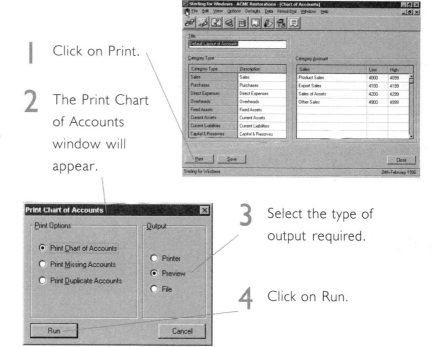

3 Select the type of output required.

4 Click on Run.

Deleting a Chart of Accounts Layout

REMEMBER

The current default layout cannot be deleted.

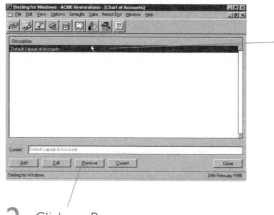

1 Click on the required Chart of Accounts layout.

2 Click on Remove.

Nominal Reports

Start the Nominal Reports option by clicking on the Reports icon within the Nominal Ledger. There are already a large number of predesigned reports available that should cover most of your needs.

Reporting can be more flexible when using the Criteria button in the Nominal Ledger window.

| Click on the Nominal Reports icon.

2 Choose the required report.

3 Click here to create a new report.

4 Click Edit to change your own report layout.

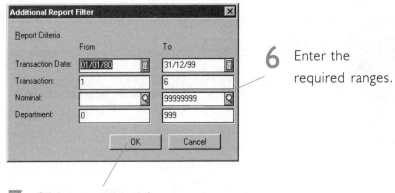

5 Choose the required output.

6 Enter the required ranges.

7 Click here to run the report.

CHAPTER FIVE

The Bank

This chapter will cover the Bank and all related accounts such as the Current account, Cash and Credit Card accounts. Topics include payments and receipts, transfers and recurring entries. Also an extensive reporting procedure is discussed.

Covers

The Bank Account 58

The Bank Iconbar 60

Setting Up Bank Account Details 61

Recording Bank Payments 62

Credit Card Transactions 63

Cash Accounts 64

Cash Account Payments & Receipts 65

Supplier Payments 66

The Bank Receipt 67

The Customer Receipt 68

The Bank Account Transfer 69

Recurring Entries 70

The Bank Account Reconciliation 71

The Bank Statement 73

The Bank Reports 74

The Bank Account

Everybody will have had some sort of dealing with a bank before, probably to open an account in which to put money for safe-keeping.

There are several different types of accounts in use today:

- The Current account

- The Deposit account

- The Credit Card account

- The Building Society account

The Deposit account is used for keeping your savings in one place to add to and accumulate interest payments for a period of time. This type of account is mostly used for individuals and not for business.

A Current account is preferred for business transactions. A number of cheques are supplied with this sort of account and this will be considered as the main account for your business. Although there is no interest earned with most business Current accounts, the possibility of requesting and getting an overdraft based on future business is possible.

Paying your creditors with a cheque has many advantages and avoids handling large sums of cash. Also in this world of modern technology many banks prefer to move towards electronic banking.

When you pay your creditor with a cheque, this cheque is an instruction to the bank to transfer an amount from one account to another. You, who signed the cheque, are the "drawer", and the person who goes to his bank to deposit it into his account is the "payee". His bank will present the cheque to the drawer's bank and they are called the "drawee".

...contd

The process of transferring funds takes time and is called "clearing" time. This period can take anything up to four or five business days. A cheque should also be crossed with two parallel lines with the words "Account payee only". This means the amount written on the cheque can only be deposited into the payee's account. If not crossed it is an open cheque and anybody can deposit it into their account. Most banks will supply cheques with the crossed lines already printed on them.

The Bank Accounts window

 | Click on this icon to start the Bank Accounts window.

2 Move the mouse pointer over the required account and click once to highlight.

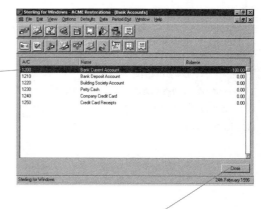

 Sterling for Windows treats both the Current account and the Building Society account as Bank accounts.

3 Click Close to finish.

The Bank Iconbar

The Bank iconbar provides features such as account record maintenance, journal double-entries, adjustments and analysis based on graphs and/or reports.

1		Open the Bank Records.
2		Open the Bank Account Reconciliation.
3		Make a Bank Payment.
4		Make a Supplier Payment.
5		Enter a Receipt.
6		Enter a Customer Receipt.
7		Enter an Account Transfer.
8		Enter Recurring Entries.
9		Run the Bank Statement.
10		Run Bank Account Reports.

HANDY TIP

Move the mouse pointer over the required icon and the description will display itself.

Setting Up Bank Account Details

 | Click on this icon to enter account record details.

2 Make any necessary changes here.

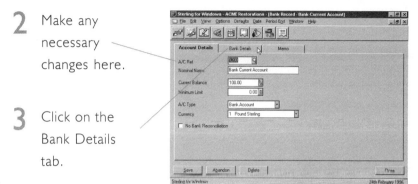

 When setting up your own Bank account use nominal codes 1200 to 1299.

3 Click on the Bank Details tab.

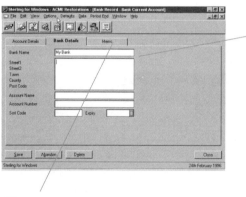

4 Enter all necessary Bank account details here.

5 Click on the Memo tab next.

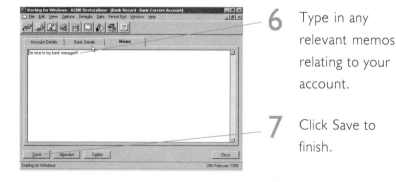

6 Type in any relevant memos relating to your account.

7 Click Save to finish.

Recording Bank Payments

The Bank Payment option should only be used for payments other than supplier payments, being any payments made against lodged invoices. (For these you should use the Supplier Payments screen.)

1 Move the mouse pointer over the required account and click once.

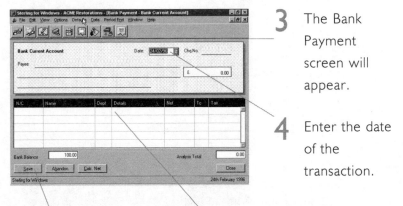

2 Click on the Bank Payment icon.

HANDY TIP

Use the Calendar button to enter the date.

3 The Bank Payment screen will appear.

4 Enter the date of the transaction.

6 Click Save to post the transaction.

5 Enter the correct nominal code and then all details such as description, amount and tax code.

Credit Card Transactions

More businesses will make payments using their business credit card. Use the Credit Card account already set up for those transactions.

You can also post credit card payments using the Bank Current account. See Recording Bank Payments.

1 Move the mouse pointer over the Credit Card account and click once to highlight.

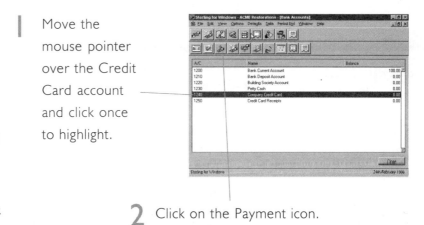

2 Click on the Payment icon.

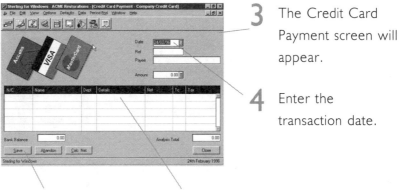

3 The Credit Card Payment screen will appear.

4 Enter the transaction date.

6 Click Save to post the transaction.

5 Choose the correct nominal code and then enter all necessary details such as description, amount and tax code.

Cash Accounts

This section is about the Cash account, more commonly known as Petty Cash. This account is a subdivision of your Bank account and is listed within your Bank option.

What is Petty Cash? On a daily basis the business may have a number of small miscellaneous expenses, such as tea and coffee or office stationery. Instead of issuing a bank cheque for such small amounts, a designated employee of the company usually controls the Petty Cash box.

In it is kept a small amount of cash to cover those particular expenses. The returned receipt for the purchase is then recorded in the Petty Cash book or in your case in the Payment screen within the Petty Cash account.

On a regular basis, maybe once a month, a cheque is then raised to replenish the Petty Cash box and is recorded as a Bank Account Transfer, covered in a later section of this chapter.

Move the mouse pointer over the Petty Cash account and click once to highlight.

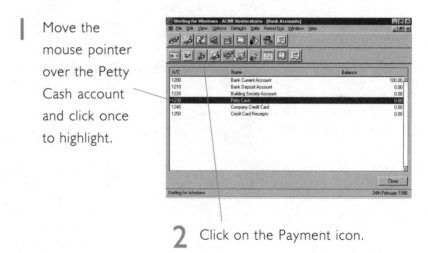

2 Click on the Payment icon.

Cash Account Payments & Receipts

Cash Payments

This screen is used to enter individual Petty Cash expenses.

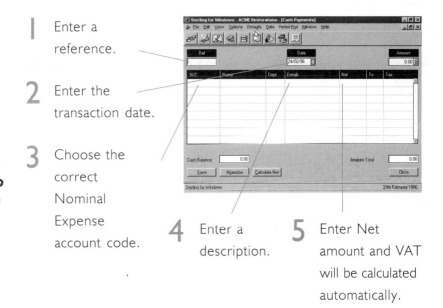

1 Enter a reference.

2 Enter the transaction date.

HANDY TIP

Use the Calendar button to enter the date.

3 Choose the correct Nominal Expense account code.

4 Enter a description.

5 Enter Net amount and VAT will be calculated automatically.

Cash Receipts

Sometimes a business will deal a lot in cash, not just using petty cash. This is when a Cash account can be used, for example, for depositing cash in a night safe. When receiving cash the Cash Receipts window should be used, followed by an Account Transfer when the cash is deposited into the Current account.

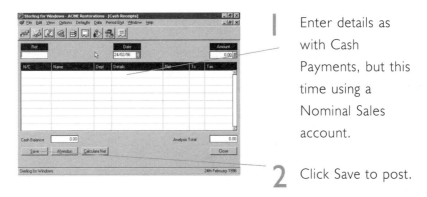

1 Enter details as with Cash Payments, but this time using a Nominal Sales account.

2 Click Save to post.

Supplier Payments

The Supplier Payment is your payment on account. The transaction of the goods purchased has already been made by entering the invoice details into the Supplier Ledger.

1 Click on the Bank Current account.

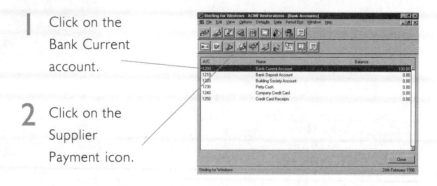

2 Click on the Supplier Payment icon.

3 The Supplier Payment screen will appear.

Use the Wizard to help you post your Supplier Payments.

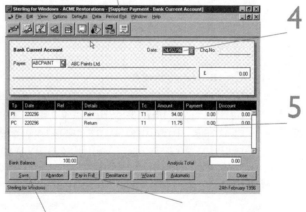

4 Enter the transaction date.

5 The previously input invoice(s) will be displayed. Click on the applied payment.

7 Click Save to post the transaction.

6 Click on Pay in Full, or type in part payment.

The Bank Receipt

The Bank Receipt option should only be used for receipts not including customer receipts, meaning any receipts pertaining to lodged invoices within the Customer Ledger.

1 Click on the Bank Current account.

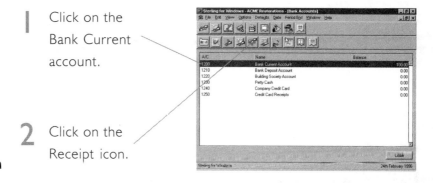

Enter the total amount in the Amount box to act as a check that all individual payments have been entered.

2 Click on the Receipt icon.

3 The Bank Receipt window will appear.

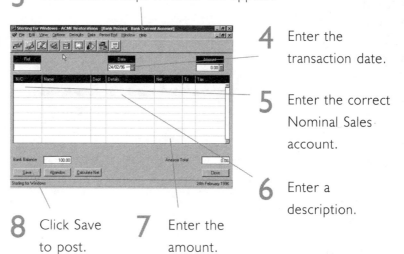

4 Enter the transaction date.

5 Enter the correct Nominal Sales account.

6 Enter a description.

8 Click Save to post.

7 Enter the amount.

The Customer Receipt

The Customer Receipt is your receipt on account. The transaction of the goods sold has already been entered by posting the invoice details into the Customer Ledger.

1 Click on the Bank Current account.

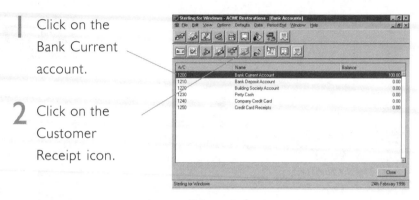

2 Click on the Customer Receipt icon.

HANDY TIP

You can use the Automatic button to allocate full payment to all outstanding payments.

3 The Customer Receipt window will appear.

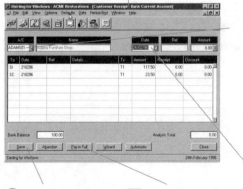

4 Type in the Customer Account code or click on the Finder button to the right of it to display the Customer List.

5 Enter the transaction date.

6 The invoice details will be displayed automatically.

7 Apply payment in full or type in part payment.

8 Click Save to post the transaction.

The Bank Account Transfer

As the heading implies, this option is used to transfer money between Bank accounts.

1 Click on the Bank Current account.

2 Click on the Transfer icon.

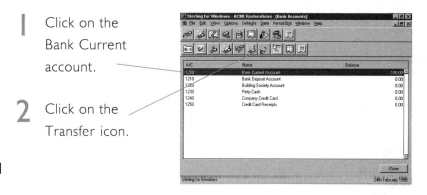

This option will only transfer values between Bank accounts, and there is no VAT included.

3 The Transfer window will appear.

4 Choose the correct Transfer account.

5 Enter the transaction date.

Use the Calendar button to enter the date.

7 Click Save to post the transaction.

6 Enter the amount.

Recurring Entries

Every month it is necessary to check recurring entries within the bank statement, such as direct debits and standing orders. They can be easily forgotten and the Recurring Entry screen will remind you. It will display itself at the start of the program if you wish it to do so.

Click on the Recurring Entry icon and then the Add button to start new entries.

Sterling for Windows will only let you post a journal credit with the corresponding journal debit, or vice versa.

1 Choose from either Payment or Receipt.

2 Choose the correct bank account.

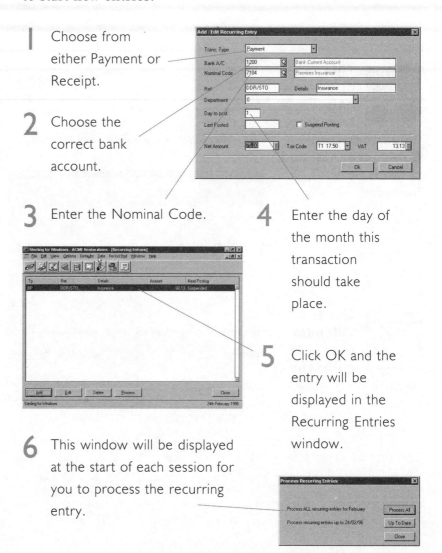

3 Enter the Nominal Code.

4 Enter the day of the month this transaction should take place.

5 Click OK and the entry will be displayed in the Recurring Entries window.

6 This window will be displayed at the start of each session for you to process the recurring entry.

The Bank Account Reconciliation

At regular intervals when you receive your bank statements you should check the bank's records with your own, comparing all transactions. This procedure is called reconciling your bank account in your books with what the bank has recorded.

It could be that you have not as yet posted the bank charges or some direct debits. But even then the two balances will no doubt be different from each other. The reason for that is that some cheque payments to your suppliers have not yet been presented to your bank and therefore do not show in your statement.

You may have already posted the payment in the Bank Supplier Payment section, and that posting would have changed your bank balance in Sterling for Windows. If that payment has not been presented by the time the statement was printed then the two account balances will differ.

Once you have assured yourself that any outstanding transactions have been made you can click on the Bank Reconciliation icon in the Bank window. Every bank transaction made will appear in front of you, and using the bank statement you can highlight them one at a time if they have also been transacted by your bank.

I Choose the account to be reconciled.

2 Click on the Bank Account Reconciliation icon.

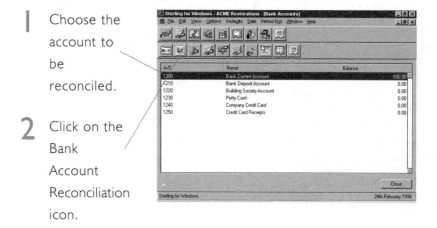

...contd

The Bank Account Reconciliation

At the bottom of the Bank Reconciliation screen a bank and book balance will appear. Once all transactions have been reconciled the statement balance in the Reconciliation window should be the same as the balance on your bank statement. This assures you that all transactions concerning your Bank account have been made.

Only those transactions not previously reconciled will appear.

1 Click on the transaction as in the bank statement.

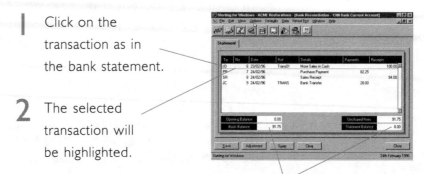

2 The selected transaction will be highlighted.

3 Check the Book and Statement Balances.

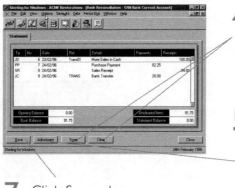

4 Click Swap to highlight all transactions or Clear to deselect all.

5 You can make adjustments to transactions if necessary.

Bank transactions will show an R when reconciled and an N when not reconciled within the Audit Trail.

7 Click Save when finished.

6 Enter the required details of the adjustment.

The Bank Statement

At regular intervals your bank will supply you with a copy of your account from their Customer Ledger showing all transactions made in your account since the last statement.

After you have finished reconciling your Bank accounts you can print your own bank statements for one or all of them, showing all reconciled transactions. That printed statement should match the statement provided by your bank.

1 Choose the account you want a statement for

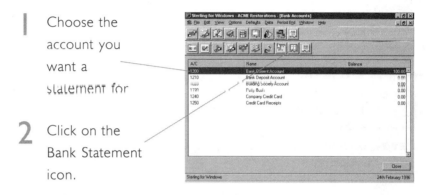

2 Click on the Bank Statement icon.

3 The Bank Statements window will appear.

 HANDY TIP

Use the Calendar button to enter the date.

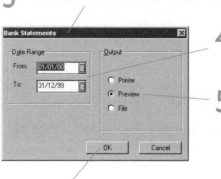

4 Enter the date range for the required statement.

5 Choose the required output.

6 Click OK to run the report.

The Bank Reports

Start the Bank Reports option by clicking on the Reports icon within the bank. There are already a large number of predesigned reports available that should cover most of your needs.

 1 Click on the Bank Reports icon.

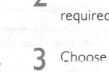 **2** Choose the required report.

HANDY TIP 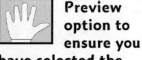 **Use the Preview option to ensure you have selected the correct report.**

3 Choose the required output.

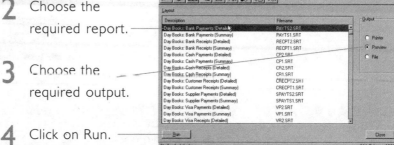

4 Click on Run.

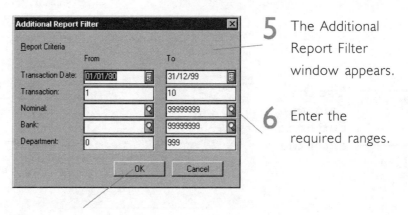

5 The Additional Report Filter window appears.

6 Enter the required ranges.

7 Click here to run the report.

CHAPTER SIX

Products

This chapter will cover products and all related topics such as detailed product control and analysis using graphs and reporting procedures, making stock adjustments and transfers.

Covers

The Product Record 76

The Products Iconbar.. 77

Product Record Details.. 78

Adjustments 82

Product Transfer... 83

The Product Reports.. 84

The Product Record

If your business concerns product sales then Sterling for Windows lets you keep records of all your sales. The Products window allows you to:

- Maintain records of all products purchased and sold.

- Control movements of products.

- Analyse product transactions.

- Maintain stock control.

From the main desktop select the Products icon.

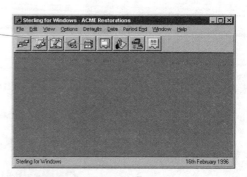

2 Move the mouse pointer over the Records icon and click once to create your first product records.

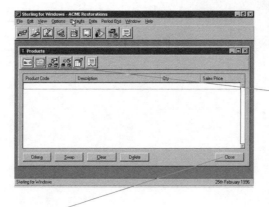

3 Click Close to finish.

The Products Iconbar

The Products iconbar provides features such as product record maintenance, adjustments and analysis based on graphs and/or reports.

1   Open the Product Records.

2   Open the Product Activity.

 Move the mouse pointer over the required icon and the description will display itself.

3   Make an Adjustment In.

4   Make an Adjustment Out.

5   Make a Product Transfer.

6   Enter Product Reports.

Product Record Details

With this option you can create individual product records and also run an analysis using graphs and activity displays. The Bill of Materials tab is useful to maintain a detailed list of products held in stock.

1 Enter a Product Code and Description.

2 Use Department, Category and Location here.

HANDY TIP **To move between tab dialogs press Ctrl+Page Up or Ctrl+Page Down.**

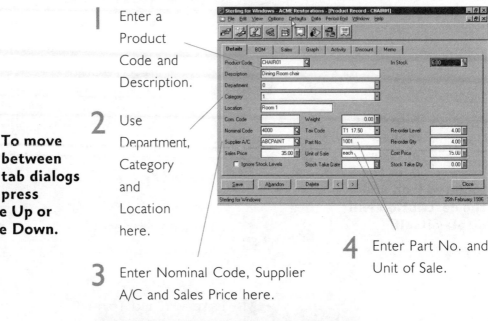

3 Enter Nominal Code, Supplier A/C and Sales Price here.

4 Enter Part No. and Unit of Sale.

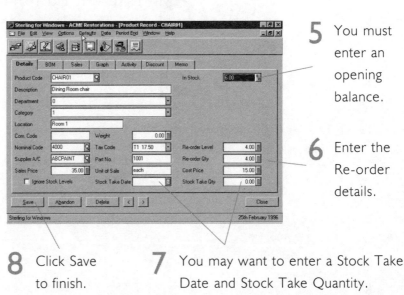

5 You must enter an opening balance.

6 Enter the Re-order details.

8 Click Save to finish.

7 You may want to enter a Stock Take Date and Stock Take Quantity.

The Bill of Materials Tab

The Bill of Materials will link a number of stock items to make up another product held in stock. The individual product items will have to be created using the Product Details option, and the BOM window will allow you to link them together to create another stock item.

1 Create your linked products first.

2 Click on Calculate to find out how many products can be made up based on quantities held in stock.

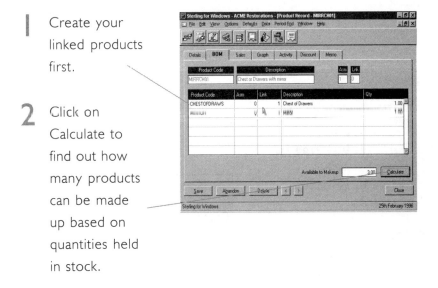

The Sales Tab

The Sales tab will inform you of the total sales history of a chosen product in monthly periods.

HANDY TIP

The Sales tab will also tell you the date of the last invoice raised for this product.

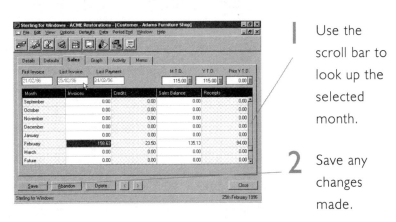

1 Use the scroll bar to look up the selected month.

2 Save any changes made.

Product Graph View

The product graph can be viewed in a number of different styles using credit, invoice and balance figures.

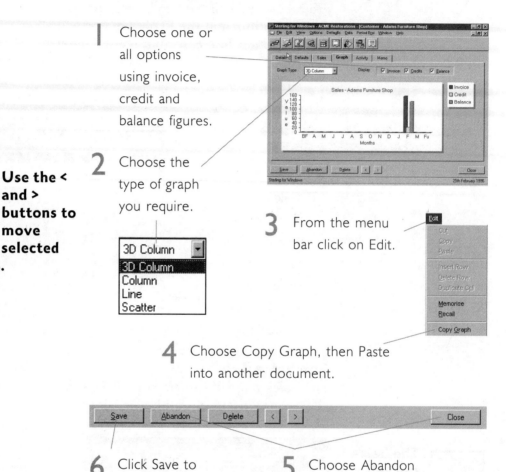

1 Choose one or all options using invoice, credit and balance figures.

2 Choose the type of graph you require.

HANDY TIP

Use the < and > buttons to move between selected accounts.

3 From the menu bar click on Edit.

4 Choose Copy Graph, then Paste into another document.

6 Click Save to keep the graph.

5 Choose Abandon or Close to finish.

...contd

Viewing Product Activity

1   Click on the Activity tab.

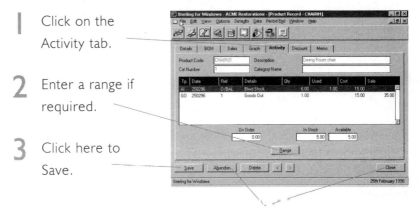

2   Enter a range if required.

3   Click here to Save.

4   Click here to abandon or close the Activity window.

You can only copy Discount tabs between Product accounts if they are of the same letter. You cannot copy Discount C to Discount D.

Entering Product Discounts

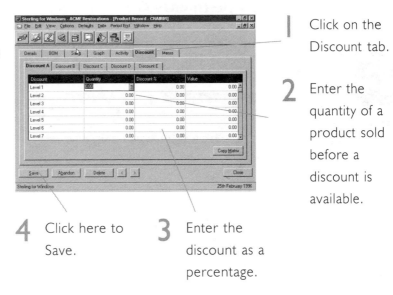

1   Click on the Discount tab.

2   Enter the quantity of a product sold before a discount is available.

4   Click here to Save.

3   Enter the discount as a percentage.

Adjustments

Adjustments In

Use Adjustments In to move stock in after a stocktake or for products for which no credit note has been raised.

Click on the Adjustments In icon in the Products window.

1 Choose the correct Product Code.

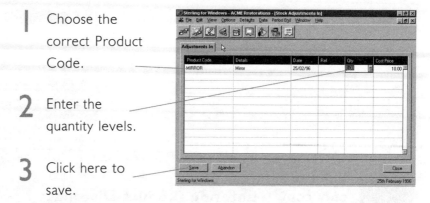

Use the Calendar button to enter the date.

2 Enter the quantity levels.

3 Click here to save.

Adjustments Out

Use the Adjustments Out option to amend your "In Stock" in case of loss or damage after a stocktake, or in case an invoice has not been raised after stock has been issued.

When you enter a reference (Ref) it will appear on your Activity Report.

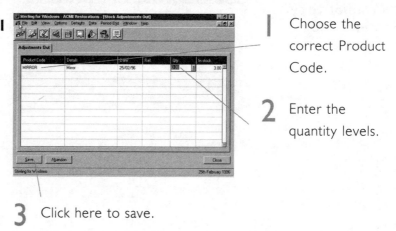

1 Choose the correct Product Code.

2 Enter the quantity levels.

3 Click here to save.

Product Transfer

Use this option to transfer all the product items to increase the "In Stock" quantity of product assemblies using items currently in stock. The product assemblies are set up by the Bill of Materials (BOM) within your Product Details (see page 79).

Product Transfer will calculate all the cost prices of all the components to determine the cost price of each assembled item.

A warning will appear if you don't have enough component stock to make up the quantity you entered.

1 Choose the correct Product Code

2 Enter the quantity levels.

3 Click here to save.

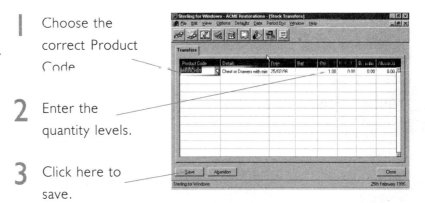

The Product Reports

Start the Product Reports option by clicking on the Reports icon in the Products window. There are already a large number of predesigned reports available that should cover most of your needs.

 | Click on the Product Reports icon.

2 Choose the required report.

HANDY TIP

Use the Finder buttons to enter the required ranges.

3 Choose the required output.

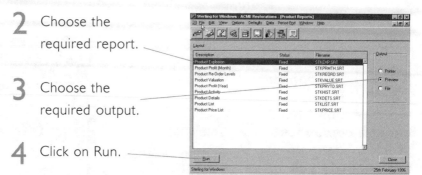

4 Click on Run.

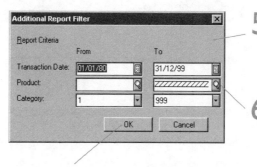

5 The Additional Report Filter window appears.

6 Enter the required ranges.

7 Click here to run the report.

CHAPTER SEVEN

Generating Invoices

This chapter will cover the generation of product and service invoices, and of product and service credit notes. It will also explain how to print batch invoices and update the ledgers.

Covers

The Invoice Iconbar 86

The Product Invoice 87

The Service Invoice 91

Printing Invoices 93

Skeleton Invoices 94

Generating Credit Notes..95

Updating The Ledgers...96

Deleting Invoices 97

Invoice Reports 98

The Invoice Iconbar

The Invoice iconbar provides features such as product and service invoice generation, credit note generation, the printing of invoices and updating of ledgers.

1   Create a Product Invoice.

2   Create a Service Invoice.

 Move the mouse pointer over the required icon and the description will display itself.

3   Create a Product Credit Note.

4   Create a Service Credit Note.

5   Print your Invoices and Credit Notes.

6   Update the Ledgers.

7   Run Invoice Reports.

The Product Invoice

When you want to record a purchase transaction concerning goods intended for resale, you must consider two different types of categories – cash and credit purchase. In the case of a cash transaction, where goods were paid for straight away, you must debit the Purchase account and credit the Cash or Bank account. In most cases, however, a business will arrange to purchase its goods for resale on account from its suppliers. This can be any period between 30 and 120 days. Therefore, once goods are purchased your business has incurred a debt and your suppliers have become your creditors.

At the same time you may sell goods to your customers on account and in this case they become your debtors. The double-entry consists of a credit entry in your Sales account and a debit entry in your Cash or Bank account in the case of an immediate sale.

When a sale on account is being transacted, an invoice must be raised informing the recipient of his or her debt.

I   Move the mouse pointer over the Invoice icon.

2   Click once to start the Invoicing procedure.

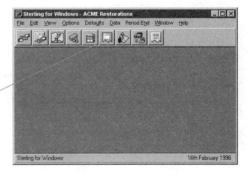

...contd

The invoice must include the following details: an invoice number, the date the purchase was made, the price and description of the goods, any VAT added (if applicable) and the terms of trading. Also the supplier's business details and the customer's address should be included. Usually there is also an order number as reference when a purchase order was raised.

REMEMBER

You can edit an existing invoice by selecting it and starting the Invoicing procedure.

1 Click on the Invoice icon, and the Invoice list will appear.

2 Click on the Product Invoice icon to generate a new invoice.

3 Enter the sales date here.

4 Enter the customer account code.

5 The customer's address details will appear here.

6 Enter the product code.

7 The description and price will be displayed.

8 Click Save to finish.

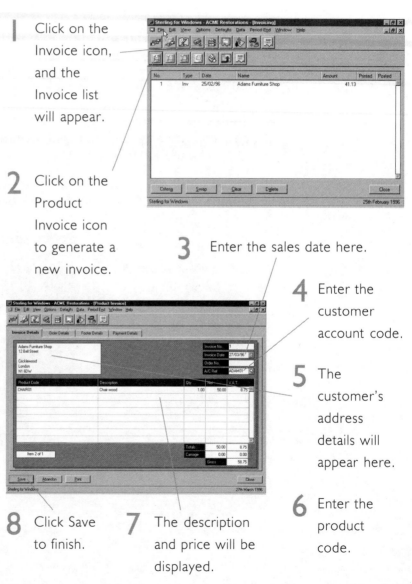

Product Item Line Dialog Box

Should you want to make one-off changes to the product sold, such as customer discounts or comments, then you can change them by entering the Product Item Line.

Changes made here will only be included in the selected invoice.

1 First move the cursor onto the Description box in the Invoice window and click on the icon to the right of it.

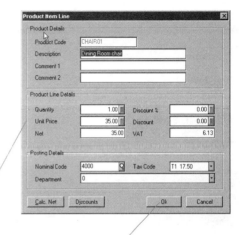

2 Make the necessary changes in the Product Item Line.

To see how the discount is made up, click on the Discount button.

3 Click OK to include the changes in the invoice.

Product Invoice Order Details

The Product Invoice Order Details tab is used to change any delivery details.

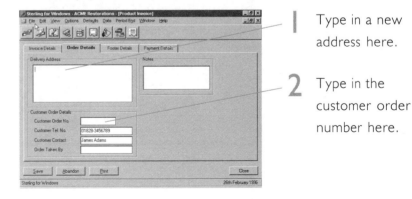

1 Type in a new address here.

2 Type in the customer order number here.

...contd

Product Invoice Footer Details

Use this tab to include carriage charges and to make changes to settlement terms and global changes such as nominal code and tax code.

Changes made here will not be included in the Customer Record.

Click on the Footer Details tab to enter the Product Invoice Footer Details screen.

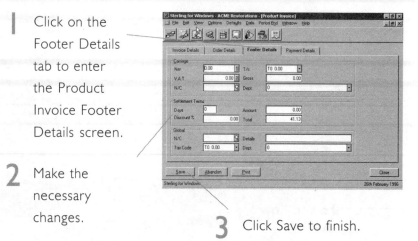

2 Make the necessary changes.

3 Click Save to finish.

Use the Calendar button to change the date.

Product Invoice Payment Details

If payment has already been received for the invoice then it can be applied within this tab.

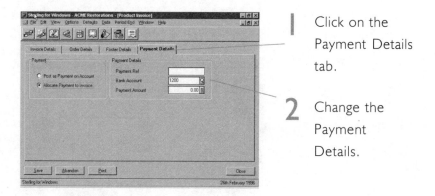

Click on the Payment Details tab.

2 Change the Payment Details.

The Service Invoice

If your business is in the service industry then you may want to use the Service Invoice option rather than the Product Invoice. There is as much room as you need to enter text; all other options, such as Nominal Code and price, can be entered individually.

1 First open the Invoicing window.

2 Move the cursor over to the Service Invoice icon and click once.

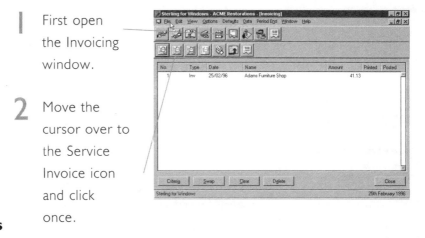

HANDY TIP

The customer's address will be displayed automatically. It can be changed if necessary, but it will not change the Customer Record.

3 The Service Invoice window appears.

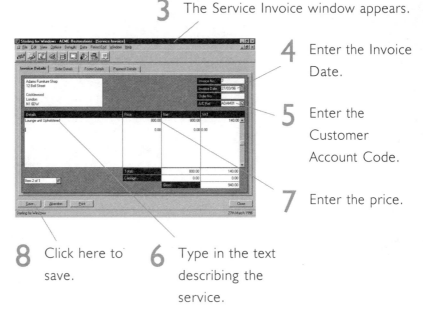

4 Enter the Invoice Date.

5 Enter the Customer Account Code.

7 Enter the price.

8 Click here to save.

6 Type in the text describing the service.

The Service Item Line

As with Product Invoices, the Service Item Line allows you
to make necessary changes in item and posting details.

**Any
changes
made
inside the
Service Items Line
will not affect the
Customer Record.**

1 Move the
cursor over the
Items box.

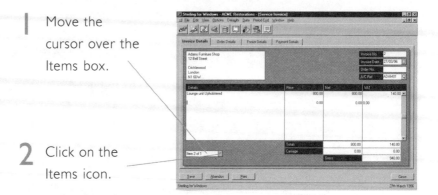

2 Click on the
Items icon.

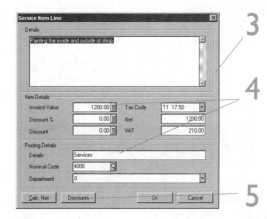

3 The Service Item Line
window will appear.

4 Change any details
necessary, such as
Invoice Value, Details
or Nominal Code.

5 Click on the Discounts
button.

6 Make one-off discount
changes if required
here.

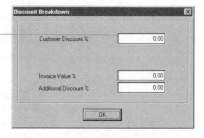

Printing Invoices

Each individual invoice created can be printed straight away. Alternatively, if you have to enter a large number of invoices in one go you can use the Print Batch Invoices option. Once the invoices have been printed the output should be checked for any errors. Printing the invoices will not update the ledgers. Therefore if errors occur you can change the invoice.

1 Move the mouse pointer over the Print Invoice icon and click once.

BEWARE **Sterling for Windows will display a warning if you try to change invoices that have already been posted.**

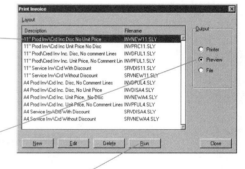

2 The Print Invoice menu will appear. With the cursor select the required invoice file.

3 Select the required output.

4 Run the print job.

5 Sterling for Windows will request confirmation that you have chosen the correct layout file.

Skeleton Invoices

Sterling for Windows has a very useful option, the skeleton invoice. When you have to generate invoices with the same layout and details you can save that information as a skeleton invoice for reuse.

Whenever you load a skeleton invoice the details will appear automatically in the boxes of that product or service invoice.

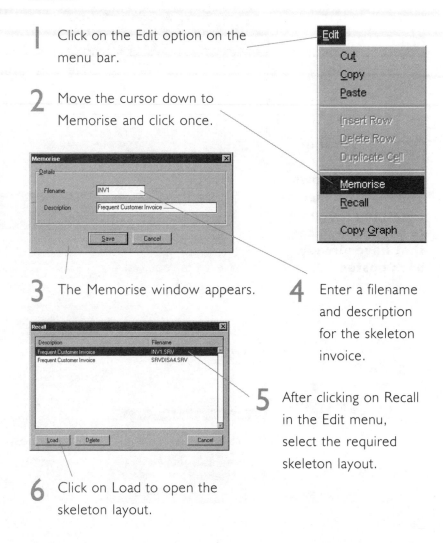

1   Click on the Edit option on the menu bar.

2   Move the cursor down to Memorise and click once.

3   The Memorise window appears.

4   Enter a filename and description for the skeleton invoice.

5   After clicking on Recall in the Edit menu, select the required skeleton layout.

6   Click on Load to open the skeleton layout.

Generating Credit Notes

Sometimes when you forward goods to your customer some of them could be faulty and they are returned to you. Or the number of items dispatched might be less than stated on the invoice.

Instead of correcting the payment to the true amount you may issue a credit note. This may be a piece of paper not very different from the original invoice. It will carry the "Credit Note" heading instead of "Invoice" and state the amount that you owe your customer. Credit notes used to be printed in the colour red, but now businesses can print from a computer using black ink.

HANDY TIP

As with invoices, skeleton credit notes can be created.

Generating a Product or Service credit note is very similar to generating an invoice, keeping in mind that the value transacted is money returned to the customer.

1   Move the mouse pointer over the Product Credit Note or Service Credit Note icon.

HANDY TIP

You can reprint your invoices and credit notes as many times as you want.

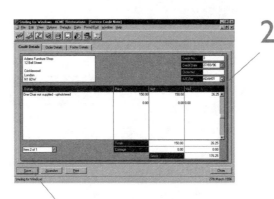

2   Enter the credit note details as you would for an invoice.

3   Click here to save.

Updating The Ledgers

Once all invoices have been generated and printed and you are satisfied that all the details on them are correct you have to update the ledgers by posting the transactions into the Customer and Nominal Ledgers.

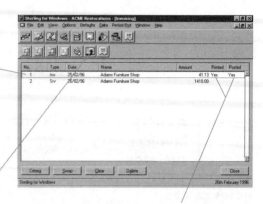

1 You may want to select individual invoices first.

BEWARE

If you change any invoice details after you update the ledgers it will not include them within the ledgers.

2 Select all invoices to be posted by clicking on them once.

4 Click on the Update Ledgers icon and then choose the required output.

3 Invoices that have already been printed and updated will display the word "Yes" here.

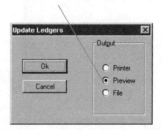

5 Preview the updated report if you want to change aspects of the layout, such as paper size, orientation and margins.

6 Click here if you want to print the report.

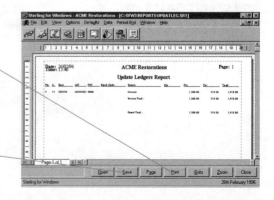

7 Click Save if you want to keep the report.

Deleting Invoices

You may decide to delete the generated invoices after the ledgers have been updated. This will not reverse the postings. When you delete unposted invoices you should use the Compress Data File option within the Disk Doctor to conserve disk space.

1 In the Invoicing window move the mouse pointer towards the invoice you want to delete.

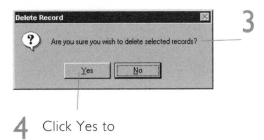

2 Highlight the required invoice by clicking the left mouse button once and then click on the Delete button.

3 Sterling for Windows will prompt you to make sure you want to delete this invoice.

4 Click Yes to delete.

Invoice Reports

Start the Invoice Reports option by clicking the Reports icon on the Invoice iconbar. There are already three predesigned reports available that should cover most of your needs.

 | Click on the Invoice Reports icon.

2 Choose the required report.

3 Choose the required output.

4 Click Run to print the report.

CHAPTER EIGHT

Fixed Assets

This chapter deals with Fixed Assets Records, the creation
and maintenance of those assets and generating Fixed
Assets Reports.

Covers

The Fixed Assets Iconbar 100

Setting Up Fixed Assets 101

Asset Valuation 104

The Fixed Assets Iconbar

The Fixed Assets iconbar provides features such as the setting up of Fixed Assets, depreciation methods and asset valuation.

1		Create and set up a new Fixed Asset.
2		Report on the asset valuation.
3		Create reports related to Fixed Assets.

HANDY TIP **Move the mouse pointer over the required icon and the description will display itself.**

Setting Up Fixed Assets

The depreciation of your business's Fixed Assets is an expense and can be offset against your profits. Fixed Assets are things such as property, plant & machinery and office equipment owned by the business.

There are four Fixed Assets accounts already set up by Sterling for Windows when using the default Chart of Accounts.

For example, let us assume that when you commenced trading you used some of your own money to get started, purchasing a workshop and a van. You spent £20,000 – that was your starting capital. You, the individual, are a separate entity from your business and you gave £20,000 to the business, this being the capital (sometimes also known as equity). On the other side the business received the same value. Because you have made a couple of purchases with the £20,000, the value is split up between two Fixed Assets accounts, the Property account and the Motor Vehicle account.

Here is how you set up your Fixed Assets accounts.

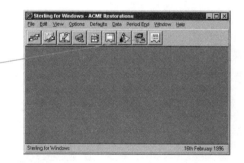

Click once on the Fixed Assets icon.

2 The Fixed Assets menu will appear, but as yet there are no assets recorded.

As already mentioned, a Fixed Asset will depreciate over a period of time and that amount is offset against your profits. When manual records were kept the depreciation was calculated annually by your accountants, but now with the help of Sterling for Windows the depreciation can be calculated on a monthly basis. This will give you an even better picture of the financial state of your business.

HANDY TIP **It is possible to delete an Asset Record at any time.**

1 Move the mouse pointer over the Fixed Asset Record icon.

2 Click once to open an empty record.

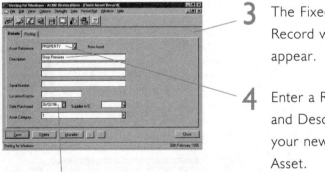

3 The Fixed Asset Record window will appear.

4 Enter a Reference and Description for your new Fixed Asset.

5 Enter the date of purchase.

Sometimes Fixed Assets may be purchased from one of your suppliers, but in this case it is not essential to create a Purchase account for the acquisition of your premises. Also a serial number and location entry are optional.

Methods Of Instalments

The first method of instalments is the reduced instalment method where the charge for depreciation is based on the percentage of the book value of the asset at the beginning of the financial year.

I Click on the Posting tab.

2 Click on the button next to the Method box.

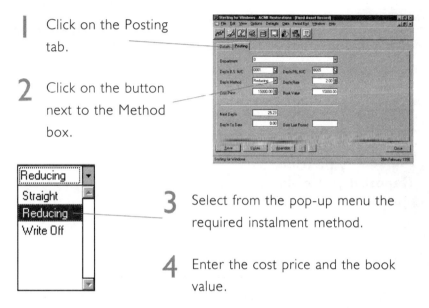

3 Select from the pop-up menu the required instalment method.

4 Enter the cost price and the book value.

Repeat the process using a Motor Vehicle account, but this time using a static instalment method. With this method the instalment will be deducted at a static or equal rate every month, based on a fixed percentage of the total value of the Fixed Asset at the start of the financial year.

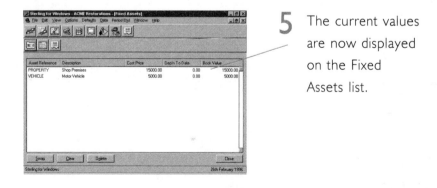

5 The current values are now displayed on the Fixed Assets list.

Asset Valuation

Click on the Asset Valuation icon to find out the current financial status of your Fixed Assets. It will display the current amount of depreciation calculated, the total cost and the current book value.

I The cost price is listed here.

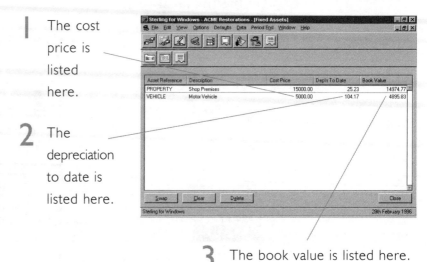

HANDY TIP **You can print the Asset Valuation** Report if you wish.

2 The depreciation to date is listed here.

3 The book value is listed here.

Fixed Assets Reports
There are two Fixed Assets reports for you to choose from.

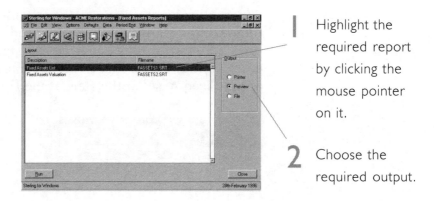

I Highlight the required report by clicking the mouse pointer on it.

2 Choose the required output.

CHAPTER NINE

Financials

This chapter will show you how to analyse your financials using detailed reporting, such as Trial Balance, Audit Reports, Profit & Loss Statements and the Balance Sheet. Reports also include a Budget, Prior Year Report, and the VAT Return.

Covers

The Financials Iconbar 106

The Audit Trail 107

The Trial Balance 109

The Profit & Loss Report 110

The Balance Sheet 111

The Budget Report 112

The Prior Year Report 115

The VAT Return 116

The Financials Iconbar

The Financials iconbar will open the following reporting procedures.

1 Open the Audit Trail Report.

2 Open the Trial Balance Report.

3 Open the Profit & Loss Statement.

4 Open the Balance Sheet Report.

 Move the mouse pointer over the required icon and the description will display itself.

5 Open the Budget Report.

6 Open the Prior Year Report.

7 Open the VAT Return.

The Audit Trail

When you first click on the Financials icon the Audit Trail window will appear, displaying the latest transactions. You can scroll back as far as there are transactions and as long as they have not been cleared by the Month End procedure.

It is called the Audit Trail because it is a report that is often requested by your auditors at the end of the year. This report will show every transaction ever made in numerical order. In the reporting procedure there are options available to define a brief or detailed report. It is recommended that after every posting session you print out a session report, forming an Audit Trail using the Filter options and entering the date of your session.

If you do clear the Audit Trail at the end of the month then you should always make a backup and print out the month's transactions before running the Month End procedure. Sterling for Windows can store up to 2,000,000,000 transactions, and providing you have enough system resources, you should never have to clear the Audit Trail. But it can slow down your system when Sterling for Windows is trying to extract transactions to process reports.

HANDY TIP

Maximise the Financials window to display as many transactions of the Audit Trail as possible, then use the scroll bar to display more transactions.

1 Click on the Financials icon.

2 The Audit Trail will appear.

3 Scroll the window to display previous transactions.

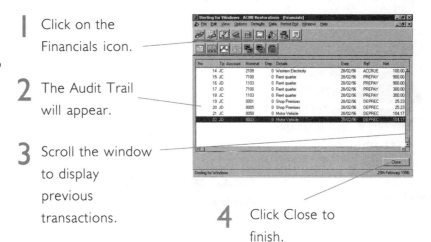

4 Click Close to finish.

The Audit Trail is a very detailed report. The column "Tp" identifies what type each individual transaction is, using the following codes:

- BR – Bank Receipt
- BP – Bank Payment
- CP – Cash Payment
- CR – Cash Receipt
- JD – Journal Debit
- JC – Journal Credit
- SI – Sales Invoice
- SR – Sales Receipt
- SC – Sales Credit Note
- SD – Discount on Sales Receipt
- SA – Sales Receipt on Account
- PI – Purchase Invoice
- PP – Purchase Payment
- PC – Purchase Credit Note
- PD – Discount on Purchase Payment
- PA – Purchase Payment on Account
- VP – Credit Payment
- VR – Credit Receipt

1 Click on the Audit Trail icon.

REMEMBER

Be as detailed as possible with your customer record input.

2 Choose the Audit Trail type.

3 Choose the required output.

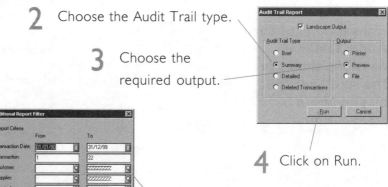

4 Click on Run.

5 Enter the Report Filter criteria and then click OK.

The Trial Balance

When you click on the Trial Balance icon in the Financials menu the program will extract all accounts that hold a debit or credit value. It will not use accounts with a zero balance.

The Trial Balance is particularly useful when checking management reports output or VAT liability reports. All Liability accounts should show a credit balance and all Asset accounts a debit balance. Also the Sales accounts should show a credit balance and the Purchase and Expense accounts a debit balance.

At the bottom the totals of the debit and credit columns are displayed and they should always balance. If they do not, then an error has occurred and this has to be investigated. It could mean the management reports are incorrect.

HANDY TIP

Sterling for Windows has Monthly Trial Balance Report options in the Reports Generator.

1 Click on the Trial Balance icon.

2 Choose the required period.

3 Choose the required output.

4 Click on Run.

5 Preview first to check the layout and then print.

The Profit & Loss Report

The Profit & Loss statement is without doubt the most important management report. It will show how the business has performed within a certain accounting period. It will start with the values of the Sales accounts within the Nominal Ledger and continue with all other accounts that have been entered in the Chart of Accounts layout.

After adding the sales values it will deduct the purchase values (from Nominal account 5000) and then the Direct Expenses accounts (up to 6999). This will produce the gross profit or loss.

It will then continue to extract the values of the Overhead accounts (from Nominal account 7000). Subtracting the cumulative amount of those overheads from the gross profit or loss amount, it will calculate the net profit or loss.

 REMEMBER **Choose the correct date range when you select the Period instead of Current option.**

 | Click on the Profit & Loss icon.

2 Choose the required Accounting Range.

3 Choose the required output.

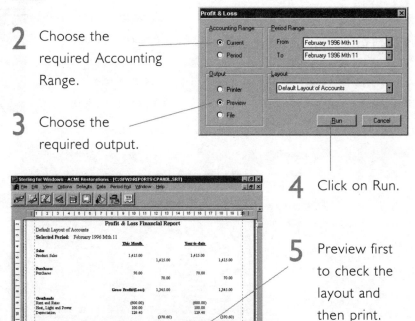

4 Click on Run.

5 Preview first to check the layout and then print.

The Balance Sheet

The Balance Sheet is not an account as such, but is included as a final report, as it is drawn at the end of the financial period.

The Report program only extracts values from the Asset and Liability accounts within the Chart of Accounts. The Fixed Asset accounts range from 0001 to 0999, the Current Asset accounts 1000 to 1999, the Liability accounts from 2000 to 2999 and the Capital accounts from 3000 to 3999.

When running the Month End procedure, make sure that the depreciation, prepayments and accruals have been posted before running the Balance Sheet Report.

The traditional method of displaying the balance sheet used to be a left-to-right layout, with the assets on the left (debit entries) and the liabilities and capital on the right (credit entries). Sterling for Windows adopts the more modern layout, this being from top to bottom. First the Fixed and Current assets, then reduced by the Liabilities. That balance should equal the Capital balance.

This conforms to the following accounting equation:

Fixed + Current Assets − Liabilities = Capital

| Click on the Balance Sheet icon.

2 Choose the required Accounting Range and output.

It is a good idea to check the Asset and Liability accounts in the Trial Balance when producing the Balance Sheet.

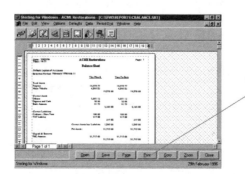

3 Click on Run.

4 Preview first to check the layout and then print.

The Budget Report

The Budget Report is produced from the budget figures that have been entered in the Nominal account. In addition to the budget figures, the ratio percentages are also worked out. Let us describe the following ratios, because they are an excellent indicator of potentially troublesome areas in your business.

Gross & Net Ratio

Once the final reports have been produced, the manager may want to determine the relationship that exists between presented figures. We call this process "ratios", highlighting those figures to be able to predict future trends and form sound management decisions on them.

We have already discussed how we come to gross and net profit. The gross profit ratio is determined by dividing the gross profit by the sales figures.

For example, if the gross profit stands at £40,000 and the sales turnover is £80,000 then the gross profit ratio is 50% ((40,000/80,000) x 100).

The net profit ratio is calculated in a similar way and expressed as a percentage. If the business's net profit is £10,000 then the net profit ratio would be 12.5% ((10,000/80,000) x 100).

Gross and net profit ratios will reflect how well the business has performed. The above example has shown a 12.5% net profit ratio; in the next accounting period the sales have gone up to £100,000 and the net profit is £12,000. The net profit ratio for the second period is 12%. Although the sales have increased in the second period, the expenses have been higher and the ratio is less than in the first period. That means the business performance in the second period has dropped. Thus, the manager is offered the opportunity to investigate.

The Stock Turnover Ratio

Stock, of course can have a great effect on the gross profit. Stock that is lying on the shelves for a long period is not turned into sales revenue and therefore reduces gross profit. The stock turnover ratio will determine the average stock held during a certain accounting period.

The Current & Liquid Ratio

The current ratio is calculated between the value of current assets and liabilities to determine the difference of what is also known as working capital. Current ratio is also sometimes referred to as the working capital ratio.

The liquid ratio is an extension of the current ratio. Because it is mainly concerned with available cash or current assets that may be turned into cash quickly, it is also referred to as quick ratio.

The Debtors & Creditors Ratio

The debtors ratio is determined by dividing the value of trade debtors and the value of total credit sales. This time the outcome is expressed as a timed period rather than a percentage. It tells you how long it takes for your credit sales to be turned into cash.

The creditors ratio, on the other hand, will tell you how quickly your business pays its own debts and thus reduces the bank account balance.

Ideally, you should minimise the debtors ratio and maximise the creditors ratio to optimum level, keeping in mind such things as valued customer relations and supplier discount offers.

1 Click on the Budget Analysis icon.

2 Choose the required Accounting Range.

3 Choose the required output.

4 Click on Run.

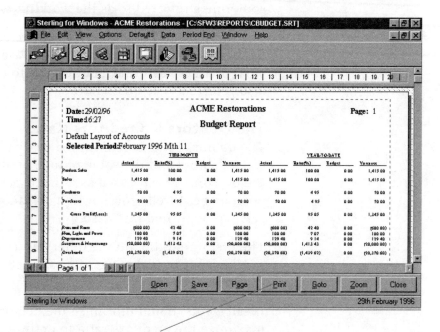

5 Preview first to check the layout and then print.

The Prior Year Report

As with the Budget report, this output will show the values of the Sales, Purchase, Direct Expenses and Overhead accounts. It will show the current month or selected period and also the year-to-date figures and compare them with the figures of the previous year.

Again, each account will display the ratios calculated as in the Budget Report. This will give you a clear picture of how the business is performing in relation to the previous year.

 1 Click on the Prior Year icon.

REMEMBER

Choose the correct date range when you select the Period instead of Current option.

2 Choose the required Accounting Range.

3 Choose the required output.

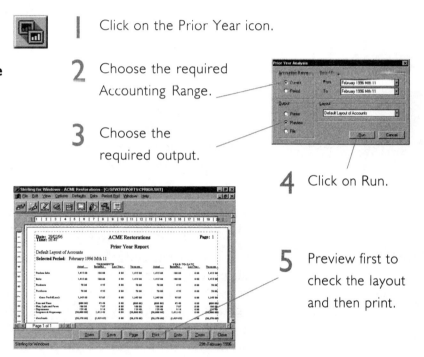

4 Click on Run.

5 Preview first to check the layout and then print.

The VAT Return

VAT is an important tax liability that many businesses are concerned with. If your business has an annual turnover of a certain amount, set yearly in the Budget, then your business must be registered with Customs & Excise.

If that is the case then Customs & Excise will provide you with a VAT number, which must be noted in all correspondence with your clients, and which will inform them that you collect VAT on behalf of Customs & Excise.

Value Added Tax is ultimately charged to the final consumer who purchases goods or services. If your business purchases certain vatable goods for the reason of reselling them then your business is not the final consumer and VAT paid can be reclaimed.

Those goods or services including VAT purchased by the business are called *input* tax. When you invoice your customer and add VAT to the price of your goods or service this is called *output* tax.

At the time of writing the standard VAT was set at 17.5%. Therefore, any goods or services bought or sold that include VAT had 17.5% added to their net value.

In the Nominal Ledger of your Sage accounting software you may have noted three accounts called Sales Tax Control account, Purchase Tax Control account and VAT Liability account. When an invoice that includes VAT is posted, that value is posted to the Tax Control account depending on whether it was a sale or a purchase.

The accumulated amounts in the Sales account comprise your *output* tax, and the balance in the Purchase account is your *input* tax.

...contd

Every three months Customs & Excise requires you to send in the VAT Return informing them of the value of your *input* and *output* taxes. When you run the VAT Return program in the Financials window, all that is required of you is to enter the process dates of the required period. The program will then calculate the difference between your *input* and *output* taxes. That difference will tell you if money is due to be paid to Customs & Excise or if money is to be paid to your business by them.

Once you are satisfied that the figures are correct, the value of sales and purchase tax should be journalised out of the Control accounts and the difference posted into the VAT Liability account. Finally, when the bank payment to Customs & Excise is made or received, the same amount will then balance the VAT Liability account, leaving a zero balance.

BEWARE

Ensure you enter the correct date range for the VAT Return. If not correct, the output from Sterling for Windows will be incorrect.

1 Click on the VAT Return icon in the Financials window.

2 The VAT Return window will appear.

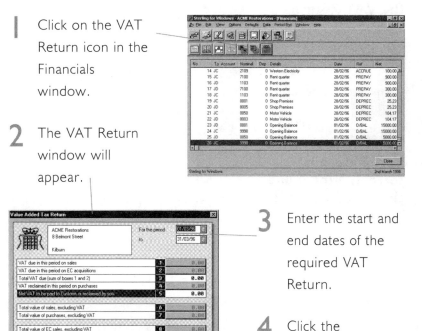

3 Enter the start and end dates of the required VAT Return.

4 Click the Calculate button.

...contd

The VAT Return program will run through the Audit Trail to check all vatable transactions. This means that your original input will have to be correct. But sometimes errors occur. This is why every time you run a VAT Return it is advisable to make a manual check and reconcile the accounts. This will ensure that nothing has been missed.

It is important to reconcile the Control accounts and to check your Audit Trail before you run the VAT Return.

Once you are satisfied that the VAT Return is correct, print it and click the Reconcile button.

After you click the Calculate button, Sterling for Windows will inform you of the amount of VAT transactions made within that period.

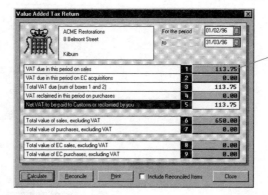

2 Click OK.

3 It is possible to analyse the breakdown of the VAT Return. Click on any of the VAT values that are highlighted.

4 Click on one of the Total buttons, and the VAT Breakdown appears.

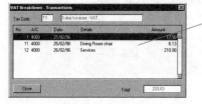

5 Double-click on an individual tax code total for further breakdown.

The Report Generator

Although Sterling for Windows already has a large number of reports within the system that should cover most of your needs, it could be that your organization has special requirements. The Report Generator will allow you to create your own reports.

Covers

Running an Existing Report... 120

Creating a New Report 121

CHAPTER TEN

Running an Existing Report

Use the Report Generator to run new or existing reports, or to change the look of your reports at any time.

1 Click on the Report Generator icon in the main menu.

2 The Report Generator window will appear.

HANDY TIP

There are nearly 70 reports available. Instead of creating a new report you can change the look of an existing one by using the Layout Editor.

3 Using the mouse pointer, click once on the required report to highlight it.

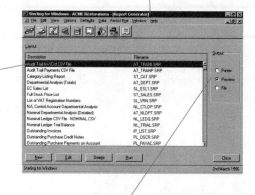

4 Select the required output (Printer, Preview or File).

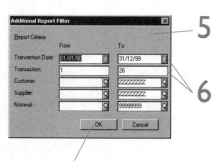

5 The Additional Report Filter window will appear.

6 Select the required ranges.

7 Click OK to run the report.

Creating a New Report

Since your organization may have individual needs when it comes to reporting procedures, the Report Generator will let you create your own report using the Layout Wizard and the Layout Editor.

| After choosing the Report Generator icon, click on New.

2 The Layout Wizard will start.

3 The Layout Wizard will prompt you for a number of details. Select the type of report that you require.

BEWARE **Use the Finish button only if you do not want the Layout Wizard to continue building your report.**

4 Click on Next.

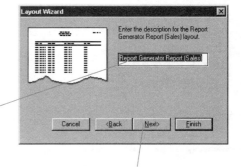

5 Now enter the name of the new report.

6 Click on Next.

7 In the following Wizard dialog box select the variables you want to appear in your report.

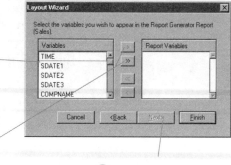

8 Click on > to select individual variables or >> to select them all.

9 Click on Next.

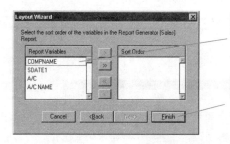

10 Next choose the Sort Order.

11 Click on Finish to end the Layout Wizard.

REMEMBER

You can always change, add or remove variables from your report at any time using the Layout Editor. Start the Layout Editor by clicking on the Edit button.

12 The Layout Editor will appear with a new document including your chosen variables.

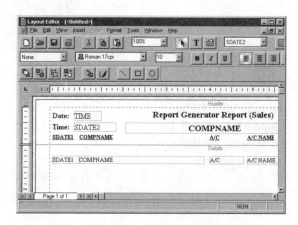

13 Make the final adjustments by moving the individual objects in the report to suit your needs, then save the report.

CHAPTER ELEVEN

Opening Balances

When you begin to use Sterling for Windows all accounts in the system start with a zero balance. This chapter will explain how and when to enter opening balances.

Covers

Introduction 124

Opening Balances and Standard VAT Scheme 126

Opening Balances and VAT Cash Accounting 129

No Full Opening Trial Balance 130

Introduction

It depends which VAT scheme you are using when entering the opening balances, but Sterling for Windows will let you do it quickly and efficiently. The opening balances are very important, because when you first install the Sterling for Windows program all accounts in all the ledgers have a zero balance.

It is acceptable to start with zero balances at any time, but if you have been in business for some time you will already have a transaction history. In previous chapters you may have noticed the option Opening Balance in the Record Detail dialog boxes of the Customer, Supplier or Nominal Ledgers. This is where you must enter the financial position of your business at the time when you start to use Sterling for Windows.

Opening Balances inform you of the following:

- Outstanding customer transactions

- Outstanding supplier transactions

- Nominal Ledger trial balance

- Stock levels

Without these balances it is impossible for Sterling for Windows to show accurate financial statements.

VAT Considerations

Sterling for Windows will allow you to account for your VAT in two different ways: standard VAT and VAT cash accounting.

The standard scheme will calculate VAT transactions whenever invoices within the Customer and Supplier Ledgers are raised, and when bank transactions are performed, including journal entries whenever tax codes other than T9 are used.

On the other hand, VAT cash accounting will only calculate VAT when customer receipts and supplier payments are transacted, when bank receipts and payments are made, or when journal entries are performed using tax codes other than T9.

Allocation Considerations

When invoices, credit notes, payments and receipts transactions are entered, they will remain visible until the corresponding debit or credit entry is made. When opening balances are entered as lump sums, it could happen that you can only part-allocate receipts or payments. But if the opening balances are entered as individual transactions then payments and receipts can be allocated accordingly.

Ageing Considerations

If the opening balances are entered as individual transactions then the Aged Balances reports will show a more accurate reading.

When to Enter Opening Balances

After entering the record details of your customers, suppliers, Nominal accounts and Bank accounts, the opening balances should be entered.

Make sure you enter the customer and supplier balances first, before you enter the Nominal accounts' opening trial balances. The customer and supplier balances will have to be cleared before entering the opening trial balance of the Nominal Ledger, because any transaction made in the Supplier and Customer Ledgers will automatically be transacted within the Nominal Ledger.

Opening Balances and Standard VAT Scheme

If you are using the standard VAT scheme then use the following to enter your opening balances.

Opening Balances for Customers and Suppliers

1 Click on the Customer or Supplier Ledger icon.

2 The Customer or Supplier Records list will appear. Click on the required record.

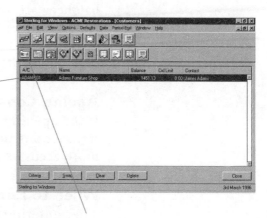

3 Click on the Records icon.

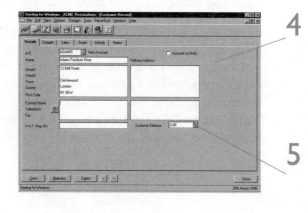

4 The Customer or Supplier Records Details dialog box will appear.

5 Click on the Customer or Supplier Opening Balance button.

...contd

6 The Opening Balance Setup window will appear.

7 Enter a reference.   8 Enter the transaction date.

9 Are you entering
invoice or credit
note details?
Choose the
correct box.

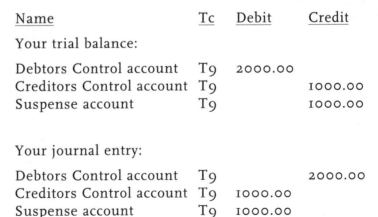

 **If you are
using the
original
transaction**
date then the
correct aged history
will be reported.

10 Click Save to post

To Zero the Trial Balance

Make sure to print a trial balance before clearing the
balances (see Chapter Nine).

Move into the Nominal Ledger and click on the Journal
icon. Using your trial balance output, identify the accounts
you wish to zero-balance. For example:

 **If you
enter
balances
for a**
number of
customers or
suppliers then use
the < and > buttons
to move between
them.

Name	Tc	Debit	Credit
Your trial balance:			
Debtors Control account	T9	2000.00	
Creditors Control account	T9		1000.00
Suspense account	T9		1000.00
Your journal entry:			
Debtors Control account	T9		2000.00
Creditors Control account	T9	1000.00	
Suspense account	T9	1000.00	

Opening Balances for Nominal Ledger or Bank Account

 REMEMBER

The balances within the Customer and Supplier Ledgers must be cleared before entering balances in the Nominal Ledger.

1 From the main window click on the Nominal Ledger icon.

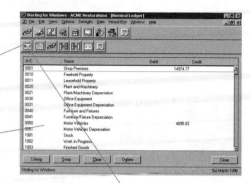

2 Click on the required account.

3 Click on the Record icon.

 REMEMBER

A liability should always have a credit entry, and an asset should always have a debit entry.

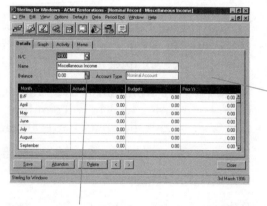

4 The Nominal Account Record Details dialog box will appear.

5 Click on the Opening Balance button.

6 The Opening Balance Setup window will open.

 HANDY TIP

To enter opening balances for product records click on the Product icon and follow the steps you would with the Nominal Ledger.

7 Enter the correct balance and then Save.

Opening Balances and VAT Cash Accounting

When using the VAT cash accounting scheme, VAT rates must be entered with every individual customer or supplier transaction, because VAT is only taken into consideration when payment is being made.

To enter the opening balances for your suppliers and customers use the Batch Invoices screen.

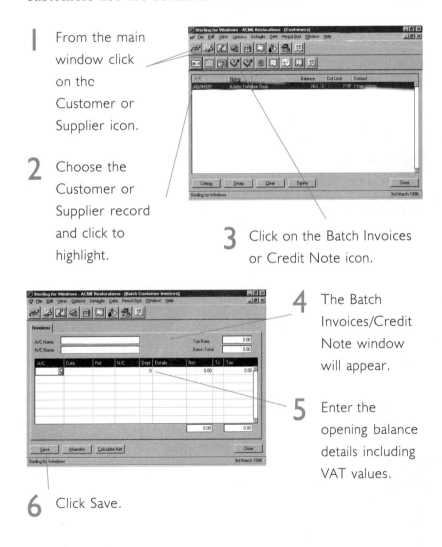

1 From the main window click on the Customer or Supplier icon.

2 Choose the Customer or Supplier record and click to highlight.

3 Click on the Batch Invoices or Credit Note icon.

4 The Batch Invoices/Credit Note window will appear.

5 Enter the opening balance details including VAT values.

6 Click Save.

No Full Opening Trial Balance

It is likely that you will not have been supplied with an opening trial balance from your accountant when you start to use Sterling for Windows. There might be some information that you have already, such as the customer and supplier list, to enter some of the record details. You may also have the bank balance from your bank statement. Such information can be entered, and the opening trial balances can be included at a later stage.

Please note that any balances entered before receiving the opening trial balance will also enter a corresponding debit or credit entry into the Suspense account. These balances will need to be adjusted when the entire opening trial balance is supplied.

CHAPTER TWELVE

Period End

The Period End option on the menu bar of Sterling for Windows allows you to do your routine housekeeping at the end of every month and at the end of your financial year.

Covers

The Month End Procedure 132

The Year End Procedure 134

Clearing the Audit Trail And Stock 136

The Month End Procedure

At the end of every month you should close off your month's transactions history by reconciling the accounts. Automatic transactions such as prepayments and accruals are processed and the Fixed Asset accounts will be changed using the Depreciation option.

If your business performs many transactions within a month's period then you might want to clear the Audit Trail, and stock files may also be updated.

You will be able to post transactions dated before or after the period once the Month End procedure has run.

Starting Month End

1. Make sure you have posted all transactions for that month.

2. Process all recurring entries.

3. Have all prepayments and accruals set up.

4. Check for any new Fixed Asset accounts.

5. Reconcile the Bank account.

6. Print all necessary product reports.

7. Post any necessary product journals.

Continue with the following procedure:

Do not forget to back up your data and change the program date to the last day of the calendar month.

It is very likely that you want to run the Month End procedure on a day other than the last calendar day of the month. This is why we must change the program date first.

1 Back up your data files.

2 From the menu bar in Sterling for Windows click on Default.

3 Click on Change Program Date.

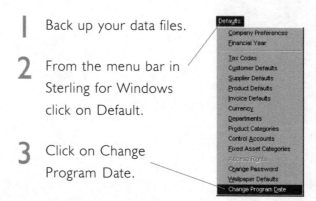

4 From the Sterling for Windows menu bar click on Period End.

5 Click on the Month End option.

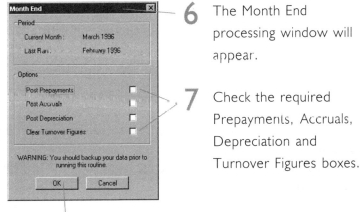

6 The Month End processing window will appear.

7 Check the required Prepayments, Accruals, Depreciation and Turnover Figures boxes.

8 Click OK to start the Month End procedure.

After the Month End program has finished, another backup should be performed (see Chapter Thirteen for backup procedures). It is best to keep a number of generations of your backup data files, with one copy on-site and another off-site for security reasons.

Finally, you can print the Management (financial) Reports, such as the Profit & Loss Statement, Balance Sheet, Aged Debtors and Creditors Analysis Reports and the Trial Balance. You may also want to run the Disk Doctor option to compress any data files.

The Year End Procedure

This option will run all your financial Year End accounting. The Profit & Loss accounts will be transferred to the Retained Earnings account and the balances of your Balance Sheet will be carried forward to the next year to give an accurate picture of the business's financial state.

Starting Year End

1. Make sure the last month's Month End procedure is completed.

 You will be able to enter transactions 2. Make sure the program date is set at the last day of the last month of your financial year.

for the new financial year before running the Year End procedure.

Continue with the following procedure:

| Back up your data files.

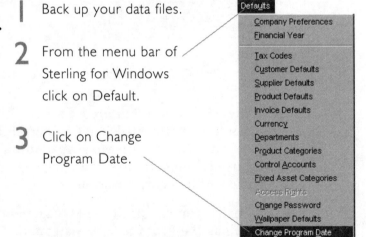

2 From the menu bar of Sterling for Windows click on Default.

 Make sure to change the program 3 Click on Change Program Date.

date to the last day of your financial year.

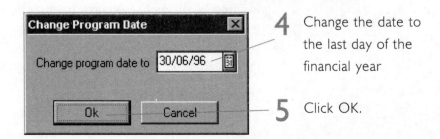

4 Change the date to the last day of the financial year

5 Click OK.

134 Sage Sterling for Windows in easy steps

6 Click on Period End from the Sterling for Windows menu bar.

7 Click on Year End.

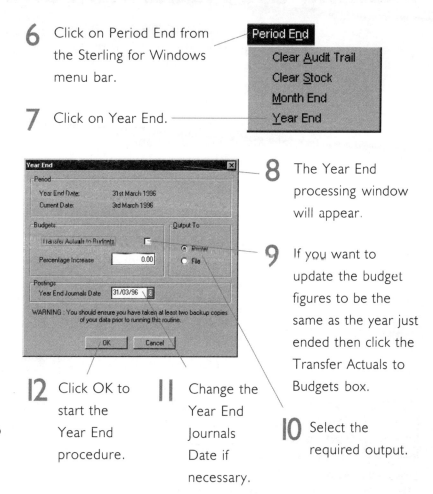

8 The Year End processing window will appear.

9 If you want to update the budget figures to be the same as the year just ended then click the Transfer Actuals to Budgets box.

10 Select the required output.

11 Change the Year End Journals Date if necessary.

12 Click OK to start the Year End procedure.

Use the Calendar button to enter the required Year End Journals Date.

After the Year End procedure has finished you should run another data file backup. You should keep a copy on-site and one off-site for security reasons.

Before you start to post transactions for the new year you can remove any unwanted customer, supplier, nominal, bank and product records. Run the Disk Doctor to compress your data files and check that the system start date for the new financial year is correct.

Clearing the Audit Trail and Stock

The Clear Audit Trail or Clear Stock option can be run when you run your Month End or Year End procedures.

Clear Audit Trail

Sterling for Windows can store up to 2,000,000,000 Audit Trail transactions and you may never have to clear the Audit Trail until such time as you feel that your system resources are not powerful enough. Whenever Sterling for Windows runs reporting procedures it extracts the necessary information from the Audit Trail. Therefore, if the Audit Trail is very large it will slow down your system.

You should also print out the Audit Trail before clearing it, and your data files should be backed up.

1. From the Sterling for Windows menu bar click on Period End and then Clear Audit Trail.

2. Transactions prior to this entered date will be cleared.

HANDY TIP **Use the Calendar button to enter the required Audit Trail and Stock dates.**

3. Click OK.

Clear Audit Trail

Clear audit trail up to [01/03/96]

Ok   Cancel

Clear Stock

1. From the Sterling for Windows menu bar click on Period End and then Clear Stock.

2. Transactions prior to this entered date will be cleared.

3. Click OK.

Clear Stock

Clear stock up to [01/03/96]

Ok   Cancel

CHAPTER THIRTEEN

Data Management

When running any computer application the proper management of the contained data is vital. Mistakes and accidents can happen at any time and therefore backup procedures are important. The management of live data files using the Disk Doctor is also explained in this chapter.

Covers

Backing Up 138

Restore 140

Global Changes 141

Importing Data 143

Disk Doctor 145

Write Off, Refund, Return 149

Writing Off Bad Debts 152

Contra Entries 154

Backing Up

It is very important that you back up your Sterling for Windows data files on a regular basis. Although it is rare that major disasters happen, many hours of hard work could be lost if no backup is available.

There are a number of strategies for backup procedures and the most common one would be the grandfather-father-son backup sequence. Depending on the volume of data input on a daily basis it is recommended that a backup is performed at least once a day at the end of session. That latest daily backup is then what we call the son generation of backup files.

HANDY TIP

It is advisable that you run a data check before you run a backup.

The next day another backup is made using a new disk. That will make the previous backup become the day minus 1 backup, also known as the father generation backup. On the third day another new disk is being used for the latest backup. Therefore, disk backup day minus 2 will become the grandfather generation, disk day minus 1 the father generation (which the previous day was the son generation), and the most recent backup will be the son generation.

If your business is a Monday-Friday operation you may want to adopt the following strategy:

	Mon	Tue	Wed	Thu	Fri
Week 1	A	B	A	B	C
Week 2	A	B	A	B	C

Using this strategy backup A is used on day 1, and backup B on day 2. On Friday a weekly backup is done called backup C. This way if an error or corruption occurs you can fall back on the previous day or the previous week.

...contd

Backing Up Data

1 From the Sterling for Windows menu bar click on Data.

2 Click on Backup.

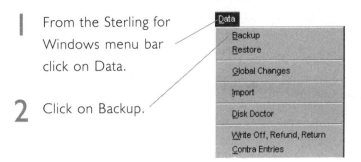

3 The Backup Data Files dialog box appears.

4 Use Setup to determine the backups' destination.

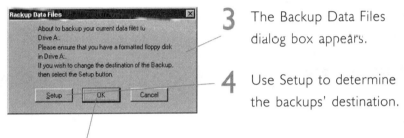

5 Click OK if the destination is correct.

7 Click OK.

 Make sure you label your backup disks with the correct generation number and date.

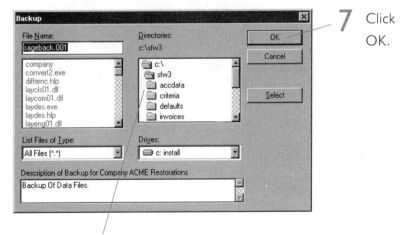

6 Choose the required destination here.

Restore

With any luck you should never have to restore your data files, but should an accident happen then the Restore procedure will take you back to the backup of your choice. How far back you can go depends on how many generations of backup disks you have.

Restoring Data

Be sure to run a data check after the completion of the Restore procedure.

I   From the Sterling for Windows menu bar click on Data.

2   Click on Restore.

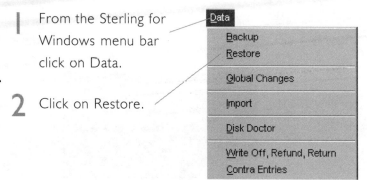

You must restore all data files; you cannot restore part of your data files, such as assets.dta only. Never use the MS-DOS Copy command to restore individual files.

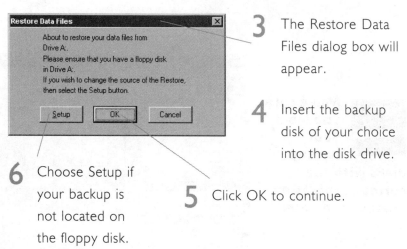

3   The Restore Data Files dialog box will appear.

4   Insert the backup disk of your choice into the disk drive.

6   Choose Setup if your backup is not located on the floppy disk.

5   Click OK to continue.

Global Changes

Should you need to change details inside all of your customer or supplier records, such as credit limits, it would be hard work having to change them individually. That is why you can use the Global Changes procedure to make those changes in one go.

1 From the Sterling for Windows menu bar click on Data.

2 Click on Global Changes.

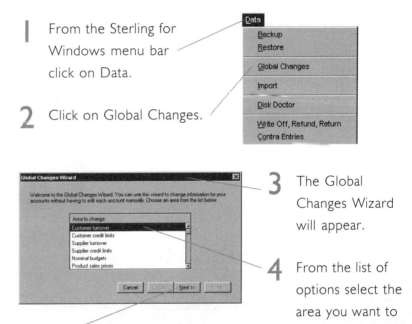

3 The Global Changes Wizard will appear.

4 From the list of options select the area you want to change.

5 Click Next to continue.

6 From the next list of options select the type of change you want to implement.

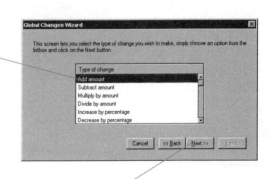

7 Click Next to continue.

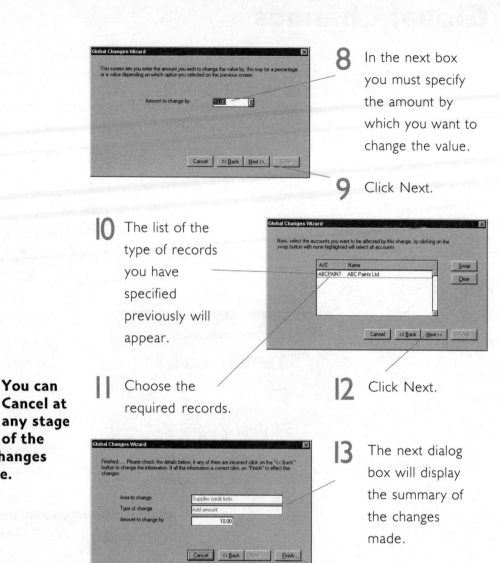

8 In the next box you must specify the amount by which you want to change the value.

9 Click Next.

10 The list of the type of records you have specified previously will appear.

HANDY TIP

You can Cancel at any stage of the Global Changes procedure.

11 Choose the required records.

12 Click Next.

13 The next dialog box will display the summary of the changes made.

14 Click Finish.

Importing Data

When you have to enter a lot of data into certain account records it can be a rather lengthy process of typing them into the records individually. Sterling for Windows lets you import files as long as they conform to a certain format.

This format is called CSV or comma separated value and has the .csv file extension. You can use programs such as spreadsheets or word-processors that will allow you to save your file in text (.txt) format.

The data record should look like this:

A0001,Computer Step,Southam,Warwickshire

Each record should be on one line and each record unit separated by a comma. The Enter key is used to start another record. Follow these rules to create your import file:

- Each unit of data is separated by a comma.

- Each data record takes up a single line.

- Each data record is terminated by a carriage return.

- Spaces are ignored at the beginning and end of the record, but not within a data unit.

- You can incorporate a comma within a data unit when enclosing the unit with quotes ("10, Belview Road").

- The data units must be entered in strict order.

- Two consecutive commas (,,) will move on to the next data unit.

- A space between two commas will delete the data unit within that record.

Importing Data

1 From the Sterling for
Windows menu bar
click on Data.

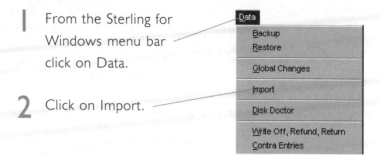

2 Click on Import.

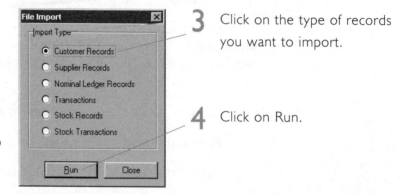

3 Click on the type of records
you want to import.

4 Click on Run.

**Be sure to
back up
your data
before
running the Import
procedure.**

5 Sterling for
Windows will
request the
name of the
import file.

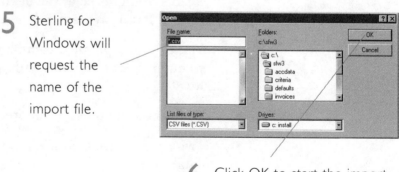

6 Click OK to start the import.

Disk Doctor

Disk Doctor has a number of useful data-management tools to check the validity of your data files. After removing a number of records at the start of a new financial year, the data file compression may return some vital disk space.

The Disk Doctor will check your data files for the following:

- Input error

- Internal inconsistencies

- Missing data

- Corrupt data

Starting Disk Doctor

1. From the Sterling for Windows menu bar click on Data.

2. Click on Disk Doctor.

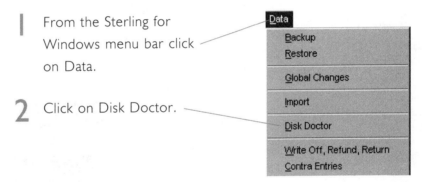

3. Sterling for Windows will prompt you to run a backup before proceeding.

4. Click Close to finish and run a backup.

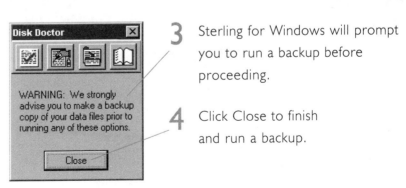

The Disk Doctor Iconbar

I Run the Check program.

2 Run the Correct program.

3 Run the Compress program.

4 Run the Rebuild program.

Disk Doctor Check

I Click this icon to run the Check program.

2 The
program
will check
all ledgers.

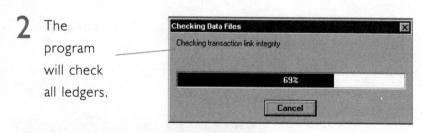

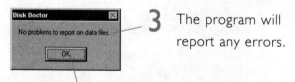

3 The program will
report any errors.

4 Click OK to finish.

Disk Doctor Correct

 | Click this icon to run the Correct program.

2 The Posting
Error
Corrections
window will
appear.

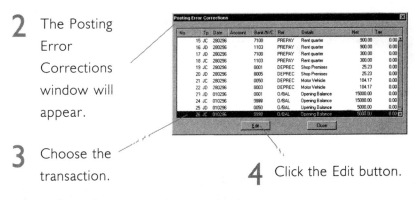

3 Choose the
transaction.

4 Click the Edit button.

 On VAT reconciled transactions the Reverse button will show instead of the Delete button.

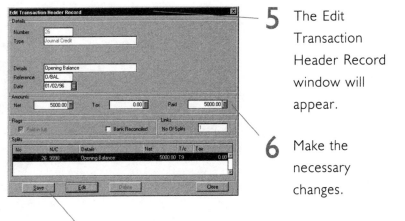

5 The Edit
Transaction
Header Record
window will
appear.

6 Make the
necessary
changes.

7 Click Save when finished.

On the Transaction Header Record you can amend the
Account (Customer & Supplier), Bank, Details, Reference,
Date and Bank Reconciled flag.

On the Transaction Split Record you can amend Nominal
Account, Details, Department, Amount, VAT Amount and
VAT Code.

On the Transaction Allocation Record you can amend the
Reference.

Disk Doctor Compress

 | Click this icon to run the Compress program.

2 The program will start and compress all data files.

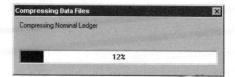

Disk Doctor Rebuild

 | Click this icon to run the Rebuild program.

2 The Rebuild Data Files window will appear.

3 Select the data file to be rebuilt by deselecting the check boxes.

4 Click OK.

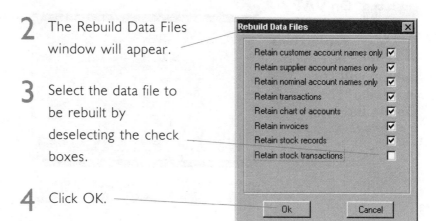

Write Off, Refund, Return

Invoice Refunds

If an error has occurred with a fully-paid invoice transaction, then it can be refunded. Use the following procedure to refund an invoice in the Customer or Supplier Ledger.

1 From the Sterling for Windows menu bar click on Data.

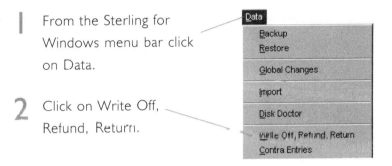

2 Click on Write Off, Refund, Return.

This option does not adjust VAT, so don't use it if you're using the VAT cash accounting scheme.

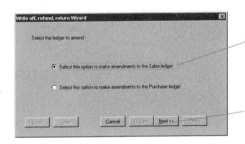

3 Choose the ledger for which the refund is intended.

4 Click Next.

5 The next dialog box will appear.

6 Click on the Invoice Refunds option.

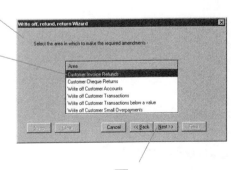

7 Click Next.

8 The next dialog box will request the required account.

9 Click on the account name.

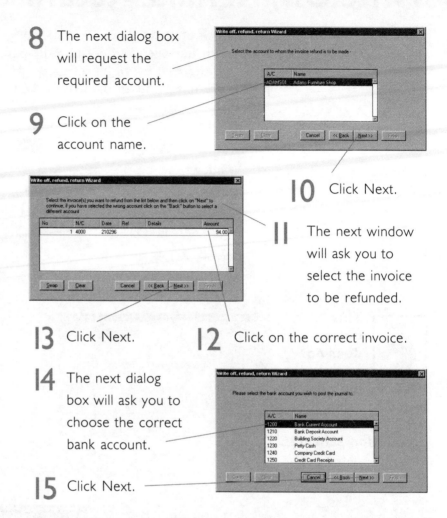

10 Click Next.

11 The next window will ask you to select the invoice to be refunded.

13 Click Next.

12 Click on the correct invoice.

14 The next dialog box will ask you to choose the correct bank account.

15 Click Next.

The last dialog box will show a confirmation screen. If you are happy with the details, click Finish to complete the transaction.

Cheque Returns

In the unfortunate situation when a cheque is being returned to you, and the bank transaction has already been posted, the Cheque Returns option will handle it.

1 From the Sterling for Windows menu bar click on Data.

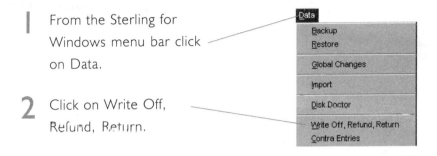

2 Click on Write Off, Refund, Return.

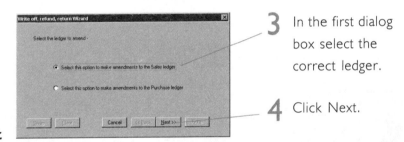

This option does not adjust VAT, so don't use it if you're using the VAT cash accounting scheme.

3 In the first dialog box select the correct ledger.

4 Click Next.

5 This time choose Cheque Returns and click Next.

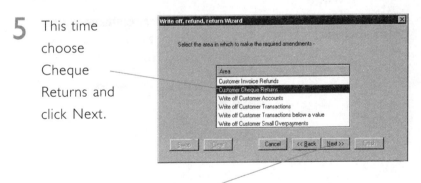

6 Complete the procedure as you would for Invoice Refunds, covered on the preceding pages.

Writing Off Bad Debts

There are four different types of bad debt that can be written off. These are: accounts; transactions; transactions below a specified value; and overpayments.

All the necessary adjustments within the Nominal Ledger are generated and the Customer and Supplier Ledger transactions are added.

Writing Off Accounts

If a customer or supplier should go out of business, then all outstanding transactions can be written off.

I   From the Sterling for Windows menu bar click on Data.

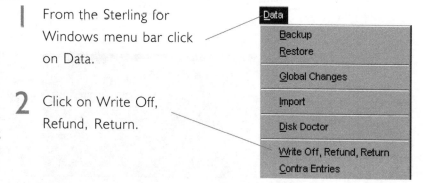

2   Click on Write Off, Refund, Return.

VAT is not taken into account when writing off transactions.

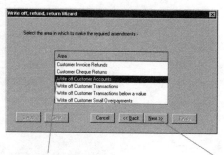

3   In the next dialog box choose the Supplier or Customer Ledger. Then click Next.

4   Click on Write Off Accounts.

5   Click on Next and continue until you come to the confirmation screen.

Writing Off Small Overpayments

Small overpayments, up to a specified amount, can be written off. Only payments on account can be written off.

1 Move from the Data menu to Write Off, Refund, Return and start the program. Then choose the correct ledger.

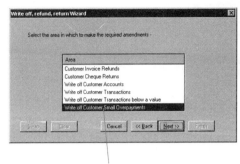

2 Click on Write Off Small Overpayment.

In exactly the same manner, you can Write off Transactions or Write off Transactions below a specified value by clicking on the appropriate heading in the Write Off, Refund, Return Wizard.

3 In the next window specify the amount below which a payment is to be written off.

4 Click Next.

5 In the next box select the payment.

6 Click Next to continue until finished.

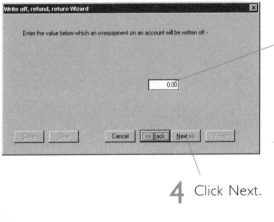

Contra Entries

If there is a need to offset an invoice, because your supplier happens to be also your customer, then you can use the Contra Entries option.

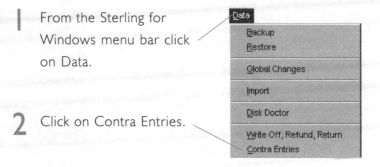

1 From the Sterling for Windows menu bar click on Data.

2 Click on Contra Entries.

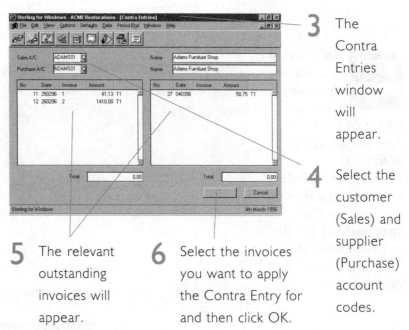

3 The Contra Entries window will appear.

When using the VAT cash accounting scheme, ensure that the selected transactions have the same VAT tax codes.

4 Select the customer (Sales) and supplier (Purchase) account codes.

5 The relevant outstanding invoices will appear.

6 Select the invoices you want to apply the Contra Entry for and then click OK.

Index

A

Accounting period 110
Adjustments in 82
Adjustments out 82
Ageing Considerations 125
Allocation Considerations 125
Asset Valuation 104
Audit trail 107

B

Backing up 138
Bad Debts 152
Balance Sheet report 53
Bank 58-74
   Account Details 61
   Iconbar 60
   Payment 62
   Receipt 67
   Reports 74
   Statements 71, 73
Batch invoices 22, 34
   Printing 93
Bill of Materials (BOM) 78, 79, 83
Bookkeeping 18
Budget 45
Budget report 53
Building Society account 58
Business transaction 14, 18

C

Capital 101
Cash account 64, 65
Chart of Accounts 44, 53, 54
Cheque Returns 151

Clear Audit Trail 136
Clear Stock 136
Clearing 59
Comma Separated Value 143
Contra Entries 154
Control account 45
Correspondence 26
Corrupt data 145
Credit Card account 58
Credit note 20, 25, 37
Credit purchase 87
CSV file extension 143
Current & Liquid Ratio 113
Current account 58
Customer
   Account 23, 51
   Activity 23
   Defaults 12
   Desktop 20
   Discounts 89
   Iconbar 19
   Ledger 18-30, 67
   Letters 20
   Receipt 68
   Records 20
   Report 30
Customs & Excise 18, 116

D

Data files 138
Data management 138-154
Debtors & Creditors Ratio 113
Debtors Control account 49
Deleting invoices 97
Deposit account 58
Depositing cash 65

Depreciation   101-104
Disk Doctor   145-148
  Check   146
  Compress   148
  Correct   147
  Iconbar   146
  Rebuild   148
Double-entry bookkeeping   21, 48-50

E

EC   11
Electronic banking   58
Equity   101
Existing reports   120

F

Father generation   138
Financials   106-118
  Iconbar   106
Fiscal year   10
Fixed assets   100-104
  Iconbar   100
  Reports   104

G

General Ledger   44
Generation   138
Global Changes   90, 141
Grandfather generation   138
Graphs   20, 33
Gross & Net Ratio   112

I

Importing data   143
Inland Revenue   18
Input error   145
Input tax   116
Installation   10

Internal inconsistencies   145
Invoice   86-98
  Footer Details   90
  Iconbar   86
  Order Details   89
  Payment Details   90
  Reports   98

J

Journal   48
Journal entry   50

L

Layout Designer   29
Layout Editor   121-122
Layout Wizard   121-122
Letters   26, 33, 38

M

Mailing labels   20, 26, 33, 38
Management reporting   18, 42, 109
Maximised profit   44
Memos   47
Missing data   145
Month End   132

N

New Report   121
Nominal
  Accounts   42
  Iconbar   43
  Ledger   42-56
  Reports   56

O

Opening balances   124-130
Opening Trial Balance   130

Options   15
Output tax   116
Outstanding invoices   24
Outstanding payments due   26

P

Password   16
Petty cash   64
Previous year   115
Printing batch invoices   93
Prior Year report   53, 115
Product
  Assemblies   83
  Discounts   81
  Graph   80
  Iconbar   77
  Item Line   89
  Records   78
  Reports   84
  Transfer   83
Profit & Loss Report   53, 110
Profits   18
Program Manager   9
Purchase Tax Control Account   116
Purchase transactions   34
Purchasing goods   37

R

Ratios   112
Reconciled transactions   73
Record details   61
Record maintenance   43
Records Analysis   46
Recurring entries   70
Reduced instalment method   103
Refund   149
Report Generator   120-122
  Layout Wizard   121-122
Restore   140

Return   149
Revenue income   51

S

Sales history   79
Sales Tax Control account   116
Sales transactions   22
Security   16
Service invoice   91
Settlement terms   90
Skeleton invoice   94
Son generation   138
Standard VAT scheme   126
Starting Sterling for Windows   9
Statement   28
Static instalment   103
Sterling for Windows   8
Stock   78
Stock control   76
Stock Turnover Ratio   113
Stocktake   82
Supplier
  Account   35
  Activity   35, 36
  Defaults   12
  Desktop   33
  Iconbar   32
  Invoices   34
  Ledger   32-40, 66
  Payment   66
  Records   33
  Report   40

T

Tax codes   11
Tax liability   116
Telephone option   27, 39
Text (.txt) format   143
Transaction   21, 107

Transaction Allocation Record   147
Transaction Header Record   147
Transaction Split Record   147
Transfer   69
Trial balance   109

U

Updating the ledgers   96

V

Validity   145
VAT   21, 88, 116
    Cash accounting   125, 129
    Considerations   124
    Liability   18
    Return   116

W

Windows   9
Write Off   149
Writing Off Small Overpayments   153

Y

Year End   134